THE SPIRITUAL LIFE

CLARIFYING THE CONFUSION

G. MICHAEL COCORIS

The Spiritual Life: Clarifying the Confusion

Front cover photograph by: Daniel Burka
Cover and interior layout by: April Beltran

TABLE OF CONTENTS

PREFACE

When I first became a believer, I had a deep desire to live a spiritual life. Since I did not grow up attending church, I did not know how. So, I began to listen to sermons and read books. I learned early that there are great differences of opinion as to how to live a spiritual life!

Most sermons I heard seem to be saying, "Get going." The idea was that if I read my Bible, prayed, witnessed, attended church, and gave money, I would be living the Christian life. While activities have a place in the spiritual life, the problem with that view is that a nonbeliever could do all those things and not even know the Lord! The spiritual life is not doing religious activities.

I was introduced to "legalism." Some sermons I heard insisted that in order to be spiritual, believers had to stop certain things. Some lists were short, such as the "filthy five," while other lists were long, such as "the terrible ten." No doubt, there are things that should be avoided, but believers can abstain from the dirty dozen and, from a biblical point of view, be carnal. The spiritual life is much more than *not* doing things on a man-made taboo list.

I heard messages on dedication exhorting believers to dedicate, rededicate, surrender, fully surrender, and consecrate themselves to the Lord. A friend told me that all I needed to do was pray every morning telling God that I surrendered all to Him that day. I dedicated myself in the morning and needed rededication by the afternoon. The spiritual life is more than praying a prayer of dedication.

During those early days of my Christian experience, I was told that my problem was that I was trying too hard. I needed to "let go and let God." I later learned this is called "quietism." That may sound spiritual, but as I discovered, it too is not exactly what the Scripture teaches. The spiritual life is not just letting God do everything while I do nothing.

I remember the day I read a book on self-crucifixion. "Ah, that is the secret," I thought, but I soon realized that self-crucifixion is impossible. I can hammer a nail in my feet and in one hand, but the other hand would still not be crucified. The spiritual life is not me crucifying myself.

Needless to say, I ended up confused. Am I supposed to "get going" or "let go?" Is the spiritual life doing or not doing certain things? Is a crisis mandatory?

In the 1980s, I developed a series of lectures on the five Protestant views of sanctification, delivering them at Colorado Christian College and later at the Church of the Open Door. That series put the issues in perspective for me, especially from a theological and historical point of view.

In the late 1990s, I preached a series of sermons entitled "A Spiritual Journey." In those messages, I explained the spiritual life using the metaphor of walking with the Lord.

In 2005, I preached another series of messages on the spiritual life. Dropping the "walk" metaphor, I covered the main topics pertaining to the spiritual life.

In 2008, I finished expounding the New Testament. Having examined each book of the New Testament as a unit, I organized the concepts of the spiritual life by explaining the major passages and topics concerning it. This material is the result. It will expound the major passages and topics of the spiritual life. It was the material I used to teach a course on the spiritual life in the Fall of 2008 at the Disciples Bible Institute and a series of messages on the spiritual life at The Lindley Church in 2010.

A name in parenthesis without a page number is the name of a commentator, who has written a commentary on the passage under consideration. Otherwise, the title of the book is given.

I wish to thank Teresa Rogers for proofreading the material. May the Lord use these concepts to enrich the spiritual life of all who read them.

G. Michael Cocoris
Santa Monica, CA

CHAPTER ONE

THE NATURE OF THE SPIRITUAL LIFE

The Bible uses a number of terms to describe the believer's relationship to Jesus Christ. For example, the term "disciple" views the relationship as one of a student learning from a teacher. The expression "abiding in Christ" pictures a believer as a branch connected to a vine. The metaphor of "walk" focuses on lifestyle. One of the most fundamental concepts is that of life. Jesus said that He came that we might have *life* and that we might have it more abundantly (Jn. 10:10). The Holy Spirit imparts new life (regeneration). The spiritual life begins with birth and grows to spiritual maturity.

SPIRITUAL BIRTH

Pardon my pointing out the obvious, but as Harry Ironside said, "We cannot live the life until first we possess it" (Ironside, cited by Wiersbe on Luke, p. 71).

SPIRITUAL DEATH

All humans are born spiritually dead. Paul says believers "were dead in trespasses and sins" (Eph. 2:1). The death spoken of in this verse is spiritual, not physical. Death is separation. As physical death is the separation of the body and the soul, so spiritual death is separation from God. All humans are born alienated from God. They are not sick; they are dead. They do not need reformation; they need resurrection.

Physical death is an illustration. Just as physically dead people have no physical life, so the spiritually dead have no spiritual life. Just as physically dead people do not respond to physical stimuli, so the spiritually dead do not respond to spiritual things.

SPIRITUAL LIFE

The solution to spiritual death is spiritual life. In Ephesians, Paul declares that God makes us alive (Eph. 2:1, 5). Life begins with birth. Therefore, it should come as no surprise that spiritual life begins with spiritual birth.

Jesus explains spiritual birth. A deeply religious man named Nicodemus came to see Jesus. Nicodemus had seen Jesus work miracles in Jerusalem (Jn. 2:23) and was convinced that Jesus was from God (Jn. 3:2). Since Nicodemus had expressed an interest in spiritual things, Jesus told him, "Unless one is born again, he cannot see the kingdom of God" (Jn. 3:3).

Nicodemus did not understand "born again," born a second time. The only kind of birth he knew anything about was physical. So he asked, "How can a man be born when he is old? Can he enter a second time into his mother's womb and be born?" (Jn. 3:4). Nicodemus was an intelligent, educated man, but with all of his mental acumen, he could not understand being born again.

So Jesus explains, "Unless one is born of water and the Spirit he cannot enter the Kingdom of God" (Jn. 3:5). The expression "born of water" is a reference to physical birth. The context of the conversation indicates that. Nicodemus just mentioned physical birth (Jn. 3:4). Hence, Jesus is saying that you must be born of water (that is, physically) and, He adds, of the Spirit (that is, spiritually). The proof that verse 5 is talking about physical and spiritual birth is verse 6. Jesus says, "That which is born of flesh is flesh (physical birth) and that which is born of the Spirit is spirit" (spiritual birth). Every mother knows that we all are literally born of water. Thus, Jesus says, "Do not marvel that I say unto you, 'you must be born again'" (Jn. 3:7). The point Jesus is making is that to enter the kingdom of God, one must be born again—this time spiritually. In other words, when Nicodemus said he did not understand the second birth, Jesus clarified by saying He is talking about a spiritual birth.

There are different kinds of life. There is plant life, animal life, human life, angelic life, and divine life. God's kind of life is eternal. When spiritually dead people are born spiritually, they get God's kind of life. They get an eternal kind of life.

The next logical question is, "How do I get this kind of spiritual, divine, eternal life?" That is exactly what Nicodemus wanted to know. He asks, "How can these things be?" (Jn. 3:9). Before Jesus answers Nicodemus' question, He rebukes him for not knowing (Jn. 3:10-12). Given his position, Nicodemus should have known.

After the rebuke, the Lord answers the question of how. How is this spiritual birth possible? First, spiritual birth is by the Son (Jn. 3:13). Jesus says, "No one has ascended to heaven but He who came down from heaven, *that is,* the Son of Man who is in heaven" (Jn. 3:13). People try to reach heaven, that is, God. They do that by trying to be religious or righteous. Jesus says it has never been done. Rather, God has reached down to earth through His Son. New life is possible because the Son has descended (a statement which demands His pre-existence, incarnation, and implies His deity), and ascended. The new birth is possible not because humans have reached God, but because God has reached down to humans.

Second, spiritual birth is by the cross (Jn. 3:14). "And as Moses lifted up the serpent in the wilderness, even so must the Son of Man be lifted up" (Jn. 3:14). In order to communicate this truth, Jesus refers to a story of the children of Israel being bitten by poisonous snakes. Those who were bitten died. Moses asked God what to do. God told him to make a snake of brass, place it on a pole and put the pole in the middle of the camp. God promised that all who looked at the pole would live, not die.

Likewise, as the serpent was lifted up in the wilderness, so must the Son of Man be lifted up. What is the parallel? As serpents caused their physical death and had to be nailed to a pole, so that which caused our spiritual death, namely, sin had to be tacked on a cross. As someone has said, "The key to heaven was hung on a nail." Spiritual life is by the cross because on the cross Christ died to pay for sin.

Finally, spiritual life is by faith (Jn. 3:15). Jesus says, "Whoever believes in Him should not perish but have eternal life" (Jn. 3:15). As the bitten Israelites looked and lived, so today when those bitten by sin look to Christ on the cross and see that He paid for their sin and when they trust in Him, they have eternal life, that is, God's kind of life. Believers have the divine nature (2 Pet. 1:4).

Gromacki says, "Eternal life begins at conversion, not at death or at the introduction of the eternal state (Jn. 5:24). It is the very life of God in which a believer can share from the moment of his regeneration. To have Christ is to have life (Jn. 14:6; 1 Jn. 5:12). The emphasis is on the spiritual quality of life, not on its timeless duration, although it does encompass the latter" (Robert G. Gromacki, *Stand True to the Charge,* p. 173).

SPIRITUAL BABES

As is true with physical birth, so with spiritual birth, all newborns are babes. Newborn babies drink milk, cry, sleep, and dirty their diapers. What are the characteristics of spiritual babes?

UNDEVELOPED

Paul says, "And I, brethren, could not speak to you as to spiritual people, but as to carnal, as to babes in Christ" (1 Cor. 3:1). Paul called the Corinthians carnal, babes in Christ. The Greek word "carnal" means "pertaining to the flesh." A babe is an infant. This is not a charge against them; babyhood is inevitable. When people are born spiritually, they have spiritual life, but they are spiritual babes. They are undeveloped. They have not developed into mature adults; they are immature.

Since they were babes, Paul says that when he was there, "I fed you with milk and not with solid food" (1 Cor. 3:2). In this context, milk is Christ crucified. Paul says that's what he preached when he was there (1 Cor. 2:2), and what he preached was milk (1 Cor. 3:2). The reason (see "for" in 1 Cor. 3:2) Paul fed them the milk of the Word and did not give them solid food was "for until now you were not able to receive it" (1 Cor. 3:2). He is not blaming them; he is simply stating a fact.

That, however, abruptly changes in the middle of verse 2. With the words "and even now you are still not able" (1 Cor. 3:2), Paul indicts the Corinthians. Being a babe is normal when people are first born, but these believers should have outgrown that stage long ago. Paul spent eighteen months in Corinthians (51-52 AD) and wrote this letter sometime later (57 AD). They had been saved for five years! They should have grown out of babyhood by now, but they had not.

Paul explains, "For you are still carnal" (1 Cor. 3:3). Some Greek manuscripts have a slightly different Greek word for "carnal" here than for "carnal" in verse 1, but the majority of manuscripts have the same word in both places. Be all that as it may, Paul is saying, "You are still carnal; you are still babes."

His proof is, "For where there are envy, strife, and divisions among you, are you not carnal and behaving like mere men?" (1 Cor. 3:3). There is a progression in this verse: envy produces strife, and strife results in divisions (1 Cor. 1:10). Paul accuses them of walking like mere men, that is, like natural, unsaved men (1 Cor. 2:14). Spiritual babes behave like unbelievers in that they are envious, contentious, and divisive.

An old farmer frequently described his Christian experience by saying, "Well, I'm not making much progress, but I'm established!" One spring when he was hauling some logs, his wagon wheels sank down to the axles in mud. Try as he would, he couldn't get the wagon out. Defeated, he sat atop the logs, viewing the dismal situation. Soon a neighbor who had always felt uncomfortable with the farmer's worn-out testimony came along and greeted him, "Well, brother Jones, I see you're not making much progress, but you must be content because you're well-established!"

UNSKILLFUL

The writer to the Hebrews tells his original readers that "by this time," they ought to be teachers, but "you need someone to teach you again the first principles of the oracles of God; and have come to need milk and not solid food" (Heb. 5:12). Since this book is addressed to believers (Heb. 3:1, 12; 6:29), not teachers, the writer is assuming that all believers ought to be teachers. Believers who have been taught ought to impart what they have learned to others.

Having not learned, they now needed to be taught the first principles of the Word again. The Greek word rendered "principles" means "fundamental elements." It was used of the alphabet. They needed to be reminded of the A B Cs of Christianity. If they were considering abandoning the faith (Heb. 3:12), they needed to review the basics.

The author explains the difference between milk and solid food: "For everyone who partakes only of milk is unskilled in the word of righteousness, for he is a babe. But solid food belongs to those who are of full age, that is, those who by reason of use have their senses exercised and discerned good and evil" (Heb. 5:13-14). Babies partake only of milk; adults eat meat. In the case of spiritual growth, spiritual babes partake of the milk of the Word, but they are unskillful in the word of righteousness. The Greek word translated unskilled means "to be unacquainted with" in the sense of being inexperienced. They did not necessarily lack information concerning righteousness. They lacked experience in putting the message about righteousness to effective use. They were inexperienced in righteousness, that is, in discerning the difference between good and evil (Heb. 5:14).

In many ways, immature believers are like unbelievers. Their behavior can be explained in terms of temperament, family of origin, and experiences. They may be moral and decent human beings. They may even be "nice." Although they may have a love for the Lord, it does not control their life. As McQuilkin says, "They yield to temptation more often than not, lusting when their body demands it, coveting what they do not have, and taking credit for their accomplishments. The touchstone for their choices is self-interest." He adds, "Scripture is not exciting, prayer is perfunctory, and service in the church demonstrates little touch of the supernatural."

Believers who ought to know better still cannot tell the difference between right and wrong. I have even had a Christian couple try to justify living together. They could not see that it was wrong.

UNSTABLE

In Ephesians 4:14-16, Paul states the ultimate purpose of gifted men equipping saints for their ministry. He states it first negatively (Eph. 4:14), then positively (Eph. 4:15-16). He says "that we should no longer be children, tossed to and fro and carried about with every wind of doctrine, by the trickery of men, in the cunning craftiness by which whey they lie in wait to deceive" (Eph. 4:14). The ultimate purpose of all ministry, stated negatively, is that believers should not be immature infants who are easily swayed and deceived. Religious quacks, who use trickery in cunning craftiness, deceive immature Christians. Immature believers, lured by the tricks and clever deceptions of religious counterfeits, are unstable. They are tossed to and fro, and carried about (literally, to swing around . . . to be carried off course), like a wave of the sea during a storm, by every new wind that blows into town.

SPIRITUAL MATURITY

DEVELOPED

Paul told the Corinthians, "And I, brethren, could not speak to you as to spiritual people, but as to carnal, as to babes in Christ. I fed you with milk and not with solid food" (1 Cor. 3:1-2a). Paul could not speak to them as spiritual, that is, as mature. He could not feed them the solid food of the Word. In this context, solid food is wisdom (1 Cor. 2:6), the deep things of God (1 Cor. 2:10), which he only gives to the mature (1 Cor. 2:6). Godet suggests that it is wisdom, the contemplation of the divine plan in its entirety from its eternal predestination to its final consummation.

In other words, had they developed to spiritual maturity, Paul would have fed them with the solid spiritual food of the Word. Spiritually mature people are developed; they have grown.

DISCERNMENT

The writer to the Hebrews says, "Solid food belongs to those who are of full age, that is, those who by reason of use have their senses exercised and discerned good and evil" (Heb. 5:13-14). The spiritually mature eat the solid food of the Word of God. They have done what the Word of righteousness says. The Greek phrase translated "by reason of use" means "practice, exercise." It could be translated "habit" (Westcott; Bruce; Guthrie). As a result of their habit of obeying the message about righteousness, they are mature; their "senses" can distinguish between good and evil.

Had the recipients of the book of Hebrews made a habit of obeying the

Word of God, they would be mature, could eat the solid food of the Word of God, and could discern between good and evil. When it came to things like eating meat offered to idols, they would be able to discern what is good and what is evil.

There are three stages of spiritual development. First, there is the "nest stage," where we depend on others to feed us. Then, there is the second stage where we are able to feed ourselves. The third stage is when we advance to spiritual maturity and are able to feed others.

DEVOTED LOVE

In Ephesians 4, Paul says, "Speaking the truth in love, [we] may grow up in all things into Him who is the head—Christ" (Eph. 4:15). Spiritual maturity is being Christ-like. It is speaking the truth in love. Three times in this passage Paul mentions love (Eph. 4:2, 15, 16). He ends with love. The ultimate in Christ-like maturity is love, but it is love that speaks the truth. It speaks the truth and it is loving all at the same time.

Mature believers are committed to the Lord, to be like Him. He is their constant companion. As a result of their knowledge of the Scripture and dependence on the Lord, they reflect the attitudes, speech, and actions of Jesus Christ. They are characterized by humility, self-control, and contentment. They are concerned for others, even allowing the welfare of others to take precedence over their own personal desires. They have an inner joy in the midst of trying circumstances and they have a loving response to ingratitude, indifference, even hostility.

The development to spiritual maturity is not done in isolation. It is done in the context of a Christian community called a church (Eph. 4:12-13). Paul says, "From whom the whole body, joined and knit together by what every joint supplies, according to the effective working by which every part does its share, causes growth of the body for the edifying of itself in love" (Eph. 4:16). Paul is using the figure of the human body to illustrate the body of Christ. Every part of the body is connected to the head—Christ. As each part fulfills its proper function, the body grows in love. Each individual part contributes to this growth in love as he does his part. As John Calvin put it, "No member of the body of Christ is endowed with such perfections as to be able, without the assistance of others, to supply his own necessities."

Charles Simpson put it like this: "I met a young man not long ago who dives for exotic fish for aquariums. He said one of the most popular aquarium fish is the shark. He explained that if you catch a small shark and confine it, it will stay a size proportionate to the aquarium. Sharks can be six inches long yet fully matured. But if you turn them loose in the ocean, they grow to their normal length of eight feet. That also happens to some Christians. I've seen some of the cutest little six-inch Christians who swim around in a little puddle. But if you put them into a larger arena—into the whole creation—only then can they become great."

Perhaps spiritual growth can only be done in the context of a Christian community because no one can irritate you like a fellow Christian. That is probably because of expectations.

SUMMARY

The nature of the spiritual life is the process of growing to Christ-like maturity in the context of a spiritual community. It is growing from acting in an unrighteous and unloving way to being righteous and loving.

Throughout the New Testament, the nature of spiritual life is *growth* to spiritual Christ-like maturity. It is a process. A number of explanations of the spiritual life place a great deal of emphasis on a crisis, such as a second blessing, entire sanctification, the baptism of the Holy Spirit with the evidence of speaking in tongues, the filling of the Spirit defined as a crisis experience, and dedication. In the experience of some believers, there may be some kind of a crisis when they began to get serious about their spiritual lives, but the New Testament knows nothing about a crisis being necessary before a believer can live the spiritual life.

Believers grow as they feed on the Word. Babes are characterized as those who can only handle the milk of the Word (1 Cor. 3:2; Heb. 5:12). The spiritually mature have grown because they have practiced the righteousness of the Word (Heb. 5:14).

Tim Hansel writes: "A close friend of mine was asked back to his forty-year high school reunion. For months he saved to take his wife back to the place and the people he'd left four decades before. The closer the time came for the reunion, the more excited he became, thinking of all the wonderful stories he would hear about the changes and the accomplishments these old friends would tell him.

"One night before he left he even pulled out his old yearbooks, read the silly statements and the good wishes for the future that students write to each other. He wondered what ol' Number 86 from his football team had done. He wondered if any others had encountered this Christ who had changed him so profoundly. He even tried to guess what some of his friends would look like, and what kind of jobs and families some of these special friends had.

"The day came to leave and I drove them to the airport. Their energy was almost contagious. 'I'll pick you up on Sunday evening, and you can tell me all about it,' I said. 'Have a great time.'

"Sunday evening arrived. As I watched them get off the plane, my friend seemed almost despondent. I almost didn't want to ask, but finally I said, 'Well, how was the reunion?' 'Tim,' the man said, 'it was one of the saddest experiences of my life.' 'Good grief,' I said, more than a little surprised. 'What happened?' 'It wasn't what happened but what didn't happen. It has been forty years, forty years—and they haven't changed. They had simply gained weight, changed clothes, gotten jobs…but they hadn't really changed. And what I experienced was maybe one of the most tragic things I could ever imagine about life. For reasons I can't fully understand, it seems as though some people choose not to change.'

"There was a long silence as we walked back to the car. On the drive home, he turned to me and said, 'I never, never want that to be said of me, Tim. Life is too precious, too sacred, too important. If you ever see me go stagnant like that, I hope you give me a quick, swift kick where I need it—for Christ's sake. I hope you'll love me enough to challenge me to keep growing'" (Tim Hansel, *Holy Sweat*. Word Books Publisher, 1987, pp. 54-55).

CHAPTER TWO

THE GOAL OF THE SPIRITUAL LIFE

(PART I)

For many, many years, I have asked believers all over America one deeply significant question: "Why did God leave you here? After He saved you, why did He not just take you home to heaven?" I have not kept records, but by far and away, the answer I have received more than any other is, "The Lord left me here to serve Him." My response to that is, if service is the reason God saved you, could you not do that in heaven? In fact, you could do it better up there than down here, because you would not have the sin nature to interfere with your service.

I have had some say, "The Lord left me here to win people to Christ." My reply to that is that in Galatians 1, Paul speaks of angels preaching the gospel. He does not need you to do that. Besides, they would probably do a better job than we do.

The reason God leaves us here is to conform us to the image of Christ. Paul informs us "For whom He foreknew, He also predestined *to be* conformed to the image of His Son, that He might be the firstborn among many brethren" (Rom. 8:29). Paul says the goal is that Christ be formed in us (Gal. 4:19). In other words, *the goal of the spiritual life is Christ-like maturity.*

The question becomes, what does it mean to be conformed to the image of Christ? What does it mean for Christ to be formed in me? What is Christ-like maturity?

Jesus is God and Jesus is man. What are His characteristics as God? What were His characteristics as man?

THE CHARACTERISTICS OF GOD

GOD

The Old Testament emphasizes that God is holy (Lev. 11:44) and the New Testament stresses God is love (1 Jn. 4:8). Around holiness can be grouped such attributes as truth, righteousness, and justice; clustered about love are grace, mercy, and kindness. Thus, the two major attributes of God are holiness (truth, righteous, justice) and love (grace, mercy, kindness).

Moses wrote, "Now the LORD descended in the cloud and stood with him there, and proclaimed the name of the LORD. And the LORD passed before him and proclaimed, 'The LORD, the LORD God, merciful and gracious, longsuffering, and abounding in goodness and truth keeping mercy for thousands, forgiving iniquity and transgression and sin, by no means clearing *the guilty*, visiting the iniquity of the fathers upon the children and the children's children to the third and the fourth generation.' So Moses made haste and bowed his head toward the earth, and worshiped" (Ex. 34:5-8). Seven characteristics of God are listed, three pairs referring to His mercy, and a single one affirming His justice. Clearly, mercy predominates, but this list amounts to two basic virtues: mercy and justice, which are similar to holiness and love.

The Psalmist said, "For Your mercy *is* great above the heavens, and Your truth *reaches* to the clouds" (Ps. 108:4). Here God's mercy and truth are praised.

BELIEVERS

As God's children, believers are to be God-like. Micah says, "He has shown you, O man, what *is* good; and what does the LORD require of you but to do justly, to love mercy, and to walk humbly with your God?" (Micah 6:8).

Jesus says, "Woe to you, scribes and Pharisees, hypocrites! For you pay tithe of mint and anise and cummin, and have neglected the weightier *matters* of the law: justice and mercy and faith. These you ought to have done, without leaving the others undone" (Mt. 23:23).

Paul says, "But, speaking the truth in love, [you] may grow up in all things into Him who is the head—Christ" (Eph. 4:15). Just speaking the truth is not the issue. Believers are to speak the truth in love. A lady once told Winston Churchill, "You are drunk." Churchill replied, "You are ugly, but I will wake up sober in the morning." That is speaking the truth, but not speaking the truth in love. Churchill did not have her best interest in mind. It was a put-down.

To have Christ-like maturity, believers must be righteous (Heb. 5:13) and loving (Eph. 4:15). Paul says, "But you, O man of God, flee these things and pursue righteousness, godliness, faith, love, patience, gentleness" (1 Tim. 6:11) and "Flee also youthful lusts; but pursue righteousness, faith, love, peace with those who call on the Lord out of a pure heart" (2 Tim. 2:22). When Paul sums up the spiritual qualities to be pursued, he mentions different attributes in these two lists, but the two characteristics that are the same in both lists are righteousness and love.

When Adam and Eve sinned, God responded with justice and mercy. He said if they disobeyed that they would die. When they disobeyed, they died spiritually, but God was also merciful. Granted, God, condemned them to pain during life and physical death at the end of it, but He permitted them to live, labor, love each other, bear children, and believe victory was coming.

The ultimate illustration of God's justice and mercy is His response to our sin. He says the wages of sin is death. Justice is making sure the penalty is paid. God is also merciful; He sent his Son to pay our sin debt. Listen to Paul explain this: "Being justified freely by His *grace* through the redemption that is in Christ Jesus, whom God set forth *as* a propitiation by His blood, through faith, to demonstrate His *righteousness*, because in His forbearance God had passed over the sins that were previously committed, to demonstrate at the present time His righteousness, that He might be *just and the justifier* of the one who has faith in Jesus" (Rom. 3:24-26, italics added).

Righteousness is doing what is right. As believers are more and more exposed to the Lord and His righteousness, they have a more and more of a desire to do what is right.

Love is doing what is best for other people. It is seeking their highest good. As believers are more and more exposed to the Lord and His truth, they have more and more of a desire to do what is loving. The most detailed description of love in the Bible is in 1 Corinthians 13. Most of the characteristics given there are what love does not do. In that passage, the two outstanding positive characteristics of love are patience and kindness (1 Cor. 13:4).

Righteousness without love is judgmental. Love without righteousness is sentimentality. Christ-likeness is being both righteous and loving. These two things are not in conflict with each other. What is right is loving and what is truly loving is right.

CHARACTERISTICS OF CHRIST

Jesus was not only God; He became a man. The New Testament makes specific statements concerning the characteristics of Jesus Christ.

TRUTH

Jesus is said to be full of grace and truth (Jn. 1:14). Still later John adds, "For the law was given through Moses, but grace and truth came through Jesus Christ" (Jn. 1:17; see also 14:5). Jesus spoke the truth. Jesus told Nicodemus the truth; He told him that he had to be born again (Jn. 3:7).

GRACE

Jesus is full of grace (Jn. 1:14). Jesus was gracious. He did not condemn the woman caught in the act of adultery. After forgiving her, He simply told her not to sin again (Jn. 8:11). He spoke the truth and yet He was gracious.

To be mature, believers must be full of grace and truth. Grace without truth is "sloppy agape." It makes one an "enabler." Truth without grace is aloof. It makes one a judge, who is critical and condemning. Grace and truth speak the truth in love. Together they make one a comforter and encourager.

MEEK

In 2 Corinthians, Paul says, "Now I, Paul, myself am pleading with you by the meekness and gentleness of Christ; who in presence am lowly among you, but being absent am bold toward you" (2 Cor. 10:1; see Mt. 11:29; 21:5). Jesus was meek. The Greek word translated "meekness" means "meekness, gentleness." It was used of a wild horse that had been tamed and was now under the control of a bit and bridle. Meekness is not weakness. A meek horse is not weak; it is strong, but its strength is under control. Like Jesus, believers are to be meek (Gal. 5:22; Col. 2:12).

GENTLE

Paul spoke of the gentleness of Christ (2 Cor. 10:1). Jesus was gentle. The Greek word translated "gentleness" means "to be fair, equitable, forbearance, reasonableness." It has been suggested that "graciousness" is perhaps the best English equivalent." My favorite translation is "sweet reasonableness" (Plummer). It is "the opposite of a spirit of contention and self-seeking" (Lightfoot). It "forbears from insisting upon full rights where rigidity would be harsh." It is "the spirit of willingness to yield under trial, which will show itself in a refusal to retaliate when attacked" (Martin).

It was said of Jesus, "A bruised reed He will not break, and smoking flax He will not quench, till He sends forth justice to victory" (Mt. 12:20). Barclay says, "The reed may be bruised and hardly able to stand erect; the wick may be weak and the light may be but a flicker." Believers are to be gentle (Phil. 4:5).

Meekness is an inner attitude. Gentleness expresses itself in outward acts.

Gentleness describes going beyond the letter of the law to the spirit of the law (Trench). "There is nothing so strong as gentleness and nothing so gentle as real strength" (DeSales).

SUBMISSIVE

Jesus said, "I can of Myself do nothing. As I hear, I judge; and My judgment is righteous, because I do not seek My own will but the will of the Father who sent Me" (Jn. 5:30). Paul said, "The head of every man is Christ, the head of woman is man, and the head of Christ is God" (1 Cor. 11:3). Jesus was submissive.

SERVANT'S HEART

Jesus said, "The Son of Man did not come to be served, but to serve, and to give His life a ransom for many" (Mk. 10:45). Paul put it like this: "Let this mind be in you which was also in Christ Jesus, who, being in the form of God, did not consider it robbery to be equal with God, but made Himself of no reputation, taking the form of a bondservant, and coming in the likeness of men. And being found in appearance as a man, He humbled Himself and became obedient to the point of death, even the death of the cross. Therefore God also has highly exalted Him and given Him the name which is above every name that at the name of Jesus every knee should bow, of those in heaven, and of those on earth, and of those under the earth, that every tongue should confess that Jesus Christ is Lord, to the glory of God the Father" (Phil. 2:5-11). Jesus came to serve.

SUMMARY

The characteristics of Christ-like maturity are righteousness and love, grace and truth, meekness and gentleness, and submission and a servant's heart.

The spiritual life does not consist of religious activities. Nor is it not doing certain things. The "dos" and "don'ts" are externalism. The spiritual life is developing Christ-like character, which means speaking the truth in love.

My wife, Patricia, worked for years as an interpreter for the deaf. One day she was explaining to me how they think and speak (through signs). Like small children, they speak what they see. To illustrate, she told me the story of a family with a deaf son. They lived next to a lady they got to know rather well. Then they moved. Several years later they returned to their old neighborhood and, among other things, visited the lady next door. After a few minutes of visiting, the son said, "Before you were thin and pretty. Now you are fat and ugly. What happened?" He spoke the truth; he needed a bit more grace.

At one point, early in my spiritual life, I had a formula for how to live the Christian life. I was satisfied, even smug, and I thought I had arrived at being spiritual. One morning as I was reading the New Testament I came upon the fruit of the Spirit in Galatians 5. As I looked at the list, I realized that it contained "patience" and I knew that I was not a patient person. I will never forget sitting there thinking, "If I am not patient, I am not as spiritual as I think I am." I had a formula, but not formation! From that moment, I have not been satisfied with my spiritual life, unless I am growing in true Christ-like virtues.

CHAPTER THREE

THE GOAL OF THE SPIRITUAL LIFE

(PART II)

Let's review. Thus far, I have described the nature of the spiritual life as a process of growing to Christ-like maturity in the context of a spiritual community. In other words, the goal of the spiritual life is Christ-like maturity. The question becomes, "What is Christ-like maturity?" Being God, Christ is holy and loving. When He walked on this earth as a human, He was full of grace and truth. He was meek and gentle. He was submissive and had a servant's heart.

That is only the beginning. The New Testament contains several lists of virtues believers need to develop (for example, Gal. 5:22-23; 1 Tim. 6:11; 2 Tim. 2:22). The items in these lists are characteristics of Christ-like maturity. Second Peter 1:5-7 is another of those lists that should be carefully considered.

VIRTUE

THE DEFINITION

Peter says, "Add to your faith virtue" (2 Pet. 1:5). The Greek word translated "virtue" means "moral goodness" and "excellence." It only appears four times in the New Testament (Phil. 4:8; 1 Pet. 2:9; 2 Pet. 1:3, 5). It is used of Christ earlier in this passage (1 Pet. 1:3). "Our word 'morality' is not too wide of the mark" (Hodges). It comes close to what the world calls character (Dave Breese). Virtue is a condition whereby any day, any night, any weekend, we can be sure that the virtuous people is living a righteous life, no matter what pressures may be placed upon them.

THE DESCRIPTION

A virtuous, moral person is one in whom there is no deception. It is possible to have desire and deception! I have known believers who in my opinion had at least, some desire to grow, but didn't. As I think about those individuals, it seems to me that there was desire, but there was also deception. In other words, there was no virtue.

A virtuous, moral person is one who says, "I am responsible." The dictionary definition of the English word "virtue" means "moral excellence, righteousness, responsibility, goodness." Instead of being responsible, we shift the blame to others.

A virtuous, moral person is one who says, "I want to do what is right." This kind of person says, "I want to do what is right *because* it is right." We do things because we want to please people or for profit. When our motive is to do anything other than what is right—because it is right—we are in danger of not doing what is right.

ILLUSTRATION

John Ashcroft writes: "Until 1997 Michael Jordan, indisputably the leading player in the NBA for over a decade, was never the highest paid player. When asked why he did not do what so many other players do—hold out on their contracts until they get more money—Michael replied, 'I have always honored my word. I went for security. I had six-year contracts, and I always honored them. People said I was underpaid, but when I signed on the dotted line, I gave my word.' Three years later, after several highly visible players reneged on their contracts, a reporter asked Michael once again about being underpaid, and he explained that if his kids saw their dad breaking a promise, how could he continue training them to keep their word? By not asking for a contract renegotiation, Michael Jordan spoke volumes to his children. He told them, 'You stand by your word, even when that might go against you.' His silence became a roar" (John Ashcroft, *Lessons from a Father to His Sons*).

Peter's list delineates the steps of growth more than any other passage in the New Testament. In it, the first step is virtue, not knowledge. Most "follow-up" programs assume that what people need to grow is knowledge. There is no question that knowledge is essential; it is the next item on the list, but it is not the next thing after faith.

KNOWLEDGE

THE DEFINITION

Peter continues, "To virtue, knowledge" (2 Pet. 1:5). Barclay contrasts the Greek word for "wisdom" and this Greek word for "knowledge" and concludes that the word for "knowledge" is "practical knowledge." He adds, "It is the knowledge of what to do in any given situation; it is the knowledge to apply to particular situations the ultimate knowledge which (wisdom) gives." He goes on to say that this knowledge is that "which enables a man to decide rightly and to act honorably and efficiently in the day to day circumstances and situations of life."

THE DESCRIPTION

Believers need knowledge of doctrine. Paul speaks of believers being no longer "children, tossed to and fro and carried about with every wind of doctrine, by the trickery of men, in the cunning craftiness of deceitful plotting" (Eph. 4:14). Without a sound, solid understanding of doctrine, you are leaving yourself open being "tossed to and fro and carried about with every wind of doctrine."

You are thinking, "That would never happen to me." Let me tell you a story. Paul went to Galatia, led people to Christ, formed churches and left town. The people were so grateful that Paul said of them, "What then was the blessing you *enjoyed*? For I bear you witness that, if possible, you would have plucked out your own eyes and given them to me" (Gal. 4:15). Nevertheless, soon after Paul left, the Judaizers came behind Paul claiming that grace was fine but ultimate justification required observance of circumcision. When Paul heard that, he wrote, "I marvel that you are turning away so soon from Him who called you in the grace of Christ, to a different gospel" (Gal 1:6-7). Wow! People led to Christ and taught by the apostle Paul were carried about by a wind of doctrine. It can happen to you.

Believers need knowledge of practical Christian living that only comes from the Word of God. Paul says, "All Scripture *is* given by inspiration of God, and *is* profitable for doctrine, for reproof, for correction, for instruction in righteousness, that the man of God may be complete, thoroughly equipped for every good work" (2 Tim. 3:16-17).

Believers need knowledge of how to be like Christ. Part of what is involved in becoming like Christ is contemplating what Christ is like in the Word. Paul says, "But we all, with unveiled face, beholding as in a mirror the glory of the Lord, are being transformed into the same image from glory to glory, just as by the Spirit of the Lord" (2 Cor. 3:18).

SELF-CONTROL

DEFINITION

"To knowledge, self-control" (2 Pet. 1:6). There are two Greek words in the New Testament that contain the idea of self-control. One, which is used in Titus 1:8; 2:2, 4, 5, 6, 12; etc., means to be sensible and self-controlled. The other, which appears here, seems to focus more on self-control (Gal. 5:22; the verb form occurs in 1 Cor. 7:9; 9:25). Green says that self-control is controlling your passions instead of being controlled by them.

CLARIFICATION

This Greek word for self-control is used in Galatians 5:22. The fruit of the Spirit is self-control, which brings up the issue of God-control. Many believers today speak of the spiritual life as if it is all God-control. That flies in the face of Scriptural statements about believers being responsible for controlling themselves.

Breeze argues that the believer is "not a thoughtless, unwilling puppet." He adds, "To say that the Holy Spirit controls us is a less-than-accurate description of the relationship between the believer and his Lord. It is rather true that He instructs us, He leads us, and we, by doing the will of God, perform heaven's purposes. The call is not for the believer to abandon himself to God. Rather he is called to responsible, thoughtful, willful obedience. Our commitment to Christ should not be presented as self-abandonment but self-control. We are not called to surrender ourselves to Him. Rather, we are 'laborers together with God'" (1 Corinthians 3:9)."

APPLICATION

The New Testament itself mentions areas that need self-control. In some of these the Greek word for self-control is used and in others, it is not.

Believers are to control their sexual desires (1 Cor. 7:9). According to the Scripture, there are two solutions to sexual sin. The first is to flee. Paul says, "Flee sexual immorality" (1 Cor. 6:18). The second solution is to get married. Paul says, "But I say to the unmarried and to the widows: It is good for them if they remain even as I am; but if they cannot exercise self-control, let them marry. For it is better to marry than to burn *with passion*" (1 Cor. 7:8-9).

Believers are to control their thoughts. Peter says, "Therefore gird up the loins of your mind, be sober, and rest *your* hope fully upon the grace that is to be brought to you at the revelation of Jesus Christ" (1 Pet. 1:13). This is a passage where the word "self-control" does not appear, but the idea is clearly there. The way to control the mind is by thinking on something else. Paul exhorts, "Finally, brethren, whatever things are true, whatever things *are* noble, whatever things *are* just, whatever things *are* pure, whatever things *are* lovely, whatever things *are* of good report, if *there is* any virtue and if *there is* anything praiseworthy -- meditate on these things" (Phil. 4:8).

Believers are to control their emotions. "Let all bitterness, wrath, anger, clamor, and evil speaking be put away from you, with all malice. And be kind to one another, tenderhearted, forgiving one another, just as God in Christ forgave you" (Eph. 4:31-32). Again the word self-control does not appear, but the concept is present.

Believers are to control their tongues. "For we all stumble in many things. If anyone does not stumble in word, he *is* a perfect man, able also to bridle the whole body" (Jas. 3:2). America is becoming a nation of angry, short-tempered people. From road rage to airplane rage, grocery store rage, and violence at youth sports events, there are emotional outbursts with unprecedented frequency.

Believers are to exercise self-control in every area of life. Paul says, "And everyone who competes *for the prize* is temperate in all things. Now they *do it* to obtain a perishable crown, but we *for* an imperishable *crown*" (1 Cor. 9:25). The word rendered "temperate" is the Greek word "self-control."

ILLUSTRATION

In a September 20, 1998 segment of ABC's news magazine "20/20," reporter John Stossel interviewed Dr. Roy Baumeister of Case Western Reserve University. Baumeister said, "If you look at the social and personal problems facing people in the United States—we're talking drug and alcohol abuse, teen pregnancy, unsafe sex, school failure, shopping problems, gambling—over and over, the majority of them have self-control failure as central to them. Studies show that self-control does predict success in life over a very long time."

The report included video of an experiment Stossel conducted at a nursery school. "By testing how well four-year-olds can resist temptation," Stossel explained, "researchers say they can predict what kind of adults they're likely to be. In the experiment, the kids were given a choice. Candy was placed on a table. If they waited ten minutes until the teacher comes back into the room, they would get five pieces of candy. If they did not wait, and give in to the temptation before the ten minutes are up, they would only receive two pieces.

"So the kids tried. It wasn't easy. Most fidgeted and looked as if they were being tortured. Some touched the candy. One boy counted the candy—maybe to remind himself that five is more than two. One girl looked heavenward as she waited, seeming to ask for God's help. Seven of the nine kids we tested lasted the full ten minutes. Most spent some time with their hand hovering over the bell." Ringing the bell meant the temptation to take the candy was too strong.

Stossel was recreating an experiment conducted thirty years earlier at Columbia University. Using a much larger group of children, the Columbia study found out which kids had the self-control to resist temptation and hold out for the full reward later—and which did not. The children were checked on over the next few decades to see which group tended to do better in life. The result of the study, Stossel said, was astonishingly clear-cut: "Kids who did well on this test years ago tended to do better in life. Better in lots of ways. Their SAT scores were higher. As teenagers, the boys had fewer run-ins with the law. The girls were less likely to get pregnant."

Self-control, then, is a key indicator of whether or not we will be successful. We can't control everything in life, but if there is one thing we can control and must control, it is our self. As Dr. Baumeister concluded on "20/20," "If we're concerned about raising children to be successful and healthy and happy, forget about self-esteem. Concentrate on self-control." (Pat Williams with James D. Denney, *A Lifetime of Success,* Grand Rapids: Revell, 2000, pp. 106-108)

By the way, Paul says, "But know this, that in the last days perilous times will come: For men will be lovers of themselves, lovers of money, boasters, proud, blasphemers, disobedient to parents, unthankful, unholy, unloving, unforgiving, slanderers, without self-control, brutal, despisers of good" (2 Tim 3:1-3). In the last days, people will be "without self-control." They will be "out of control."

ENDURANCE

DEFINITION
"To self-control, perseverance" (2 Pet. 1:6) The Greek word rendered "perseverance" means "endurance." It is made up of two Greek words: "under" and "to stay, remain, abide." Endurance is remaining steadfast under pressure. Mayor points to an interesting passage in Aristotle where self-control and endurance are contrasted. "Self-control," says Aristotle, "is concerned with pleasures... and endurance with sorrows; for the man who can endure and put up with hardships, he is the real example of endurance." Barclay says it "is the brave and courageous acceptance of everything that life can do to us, and the transmuting of even the worst event into another step on the upward way."

THE DESCRIPTION

It is said of Jesus, by the writer to the Hebrews, that for the joy that was set before Him, He *endured* the cross, despising the shame (Heb. 12:2, italics added). Paul said, "So that we ourselves boast of you among the churches of God for your patience and faith in all your persecutions and tribulations that you endure" (2 Thess.1:4; see Rev. 13:10; 14:12). Paul speaks of "enduring the same sufferings which we also suffer" (2 Cor. 1:6). The writer to the Hebrews says his readers "endured a great struggle with sufferings" (Heb. 10:32) and Peter says, "For what credit *is it* if, when you are beaten for your faults, you take it patiently? But when you do good and suffer, if you take it patiently, this *is* commendable before God" (1 Pet. 2:20).

ILLUSTRATION

One of the greatest illustrations of endurance concerns a politician. Twice he failed in business. He ran for the legislature and was defeated. He ran for Congress and did not make it. He ran for the Senate and was not elected. Then he lost in a campaign for the vice presidency. Finally, he ran for president of the United States. He experienced failure and setbacks, but he endured. His name was Abraham Lincoln.

GODLINESS

THE DEFINITION

"To perseverance, godliness" (2 Pet. 1:6). The word translated "godliness" means "reverence" (2 Pet. 1:3). Believers are to endure with an attitude of reverence toward God. They are to be aware of God in every aspect of life (Green). Hodges says that while in everyday use this word suggested "piety, godliness, religion and reverence, loyalty, and fear of God, in the New Testament, it seems to have definite overtones of the awe in which God should be held."

THE DESCRIPTION

We should be aware of the Lord at the beginning of the day. Someone has said, "I used to write in my daily calendar '7-7:30 a.m. Prayer,' but many times I passed that up. It was one more thing to pass by that day. Now I write '7-7:30 a.m. God.' Somehow that's a little harder to neglect" (Don Postema).

We should be aware of the Lord throughout the day. Warren Wiersbe says that people with this quality of character live above the petty things of life, the passions and pleasures that control the lives of others. They seek to do the will of God and as they do, they also seek the welfare of others.

We should be aware of the Lord during difficult days. C. S. Lewis said, "God whispers in our pleasures, but shouts in pain." Zane C. Hodges suggests that out of the trials of life can come "a deepening of our reverence and awe for the living God. Not only can we come to acknowledge His sovereign control over our lives, including His right to send us hard times, but we can also learn to praise Him for the mercies He grants in our deepest times of need. Such attitudes are a part of the humble reverence for our Maker."

ILLUSTRATION
Vance Havner related the story of an elderly lady who was greatly disturbed by her many troubles both real and imaginary. Finally, she was told in a kindly way by her family, "Grandma, we've done all we can for you. You'll just have to trust God for the rest." A look of utter despair spread over her face as she replied, "Oh, dear, has it come to that?" Havner commented, "It always comes to that, so we might as well begin with that!"

BROTHERLY LOVE

THE MEANING
"To godliness, brotherly kindness" (2 Pet. 1:7) The Greek word, translated "brotherly kindness" is actually the Greek word for brotherly love. The Greek word denotes "warm brotherly affection."

THE APPLICATION
"When we have brotherly love, we love because of our likenesses to others; but with *agape* love, we love in spite of the differences we have" (Wiersbe).

LOVE

THE MEANING
"And to brotherly kindness, love" (2 Pet. 1:7) The Greek word for love is not an emotion; it is an act of the will, whereby one seeks another's well-being. Michael Green defines it as "a deliberate desire for the highest good of the one loved, which shows itself in sacrificial action for that person's good." Green also

says that in friendship the partners seek mutual solace; in sexual love, mutual satisfaction. In both cases feelings are aroused because of what the loved one is. With love (agape) it is the reverse. God's love (agape) is "evoked not by what we are, but by what He is. It has its origin in the agent, not in the object. It is not that 'we are lovable,' but that He is love."

THE APPLICATION
Love is the greatest Christian virtue (1 Cor. 13:13). It is the crowning achievement of faith and therefore the appropriate climax in character development. The fact that brotherly love precedes love indicates that love here is toward not just the brethren, but to all (Mayor; Hodges). It is not restricted to fellow believers. Hodges observes, "Like God Himself (John 3:16), we are to love the unsaved. If and when we do, evangelistic efforts will be far more than obedience to the Great Commission."

SUMMARY

Christ-like maturity includes being virtuous, having knowledge, self-control, endurance, godliness, brotherly love, and sacrificial love.

Joseph Mayor says that to faith "must be added (1) Moral strength which enables a man to do what he knows to be right; (2) Spiritual discernment; (3) Self-control by which a man resists temptation; (4) Endurance by which he bears up under persecution or adversity; (5) right feeling and behavior towards God, (6) toward the brethren, (7) towards all."

How do you measure up, compared to this standard of Christ-likeness? As others see us, they should see Christ-like maturity in us. What would your mate, children, friends, co workers say?

First-graders were asked to draw a picture of God in their Sunday school class. Their finished products contained some interesting theology. One child depicted God in the form of a brightly colored rainbow. Another presented Him as an old man coming out of the clouds. An intense little boy drew God with a remarkable resemblance to Superman. The best snapshot came from a little girl. She said, "I didn't know what God looked like, so I just drew a picture of my daddy." When we live godly lives, people will see God.

CHAPTER FOUR

THE GOAL OF THE SPIRITUAL LIFE
(PART III)

When a professional football team assembles for their first preseason practice, their goal is to win the Super Bowl. When you go on a trip, you know the destination before you start. When I sit down with someone who is seeking pastoral counseling, one of the first things I try to establish is the goal. Likewise, in our spiritual lives, we need to know where we are headed.

As we have seen, the goal of the spiritual life is Christ-like maturity. I have described it as righteousness and love, as grace and truth, as meekness and gentleness, as being submissive and having a servant's heart. I have also suggested that the various lists of virtues in the New Testament, such as the one in 2 Peter 1:5-7, could be added to a description of Christ-like maturity. These are characteristics of Christ-likeness that are not specifically mentioned of Him but are true of the mature believers. This is not an exhaustive list. As I have studied the New Testament, I have noticed virtues not in the lists that could be called characteristics of Christ-like maturity. Here some of those.

SENSIBLE

DEFINITION
After I graduated from seminary, I began studying the Bible book by book. The first book I studied in depth was Titus. As I worked my way through that book, I bumped into one word again and again. It is translated "sober-minded" in Titus 1:8, "temperate" in Titus 2:2, "discreet" in Titus 2:5, "sober-minded" in Titus 2:6, and "soberly" in Titus 2:12. The elders, older men, younger women, younger men, and everyone are exhorted to possess this virtue. It is part of Christ-like maturity.

It is a very interesting word. The various forms of it (noun, verb, and adverb) appear sixteen times in the New Testament. It is rich in meaning. These words mean "of a sound mind, sane, sensible, good sense, to be in one's right mind, self-controlled, sober-minded, be reasonable, serious, keep one's mind." One ancient author said it was the opposite of madness. In fact, it is used that way in the New Testament (Mk. 5:15; Lk. 8:35).

In the New Testament, the Greek word for "sensible" is translated a number of different ways. In 2 Timothy 1:7, Paul says that God has given us a spirit of a "sound mind." In Romans 12:3, he says that believers are to "think soberly." In Titus 2:12, he says that all believers are to "live soberly."

There are several shades of meaning in this Greek term for which there is no one precise English equivalent. One scholar has stated that a translation is almost impossible. All attempts prove too narrow. He concludes that one can only hope to describe its meaning by certain catch words (*Theological Dictionary of New Testament Words*, p. 1,097-99).

The basic ingredient is soundness of mind, good sense, sanity. Such a person has balanced judgment. This Greek word also contains the nuance of self-control, self-restraint, and self-discipline. This kind of person is temperate and discreet, or, as has been said, this individual has a "measured and orderly life." Being sane, sensible, sober-minded, and self-controlled seems to say it all. Basically, however, the essence of the concept consists of two elements: sensibility and self-control.

DESCRIPTION

Commenting on one of the noun forms of this word, R. C. Trench says, "It is properly the condition of an entire command over the passions and desires, so that they receive no further allowance than that which the law and right reason admit and approve." He quotes Jeremy Taylor, who said, "It is reason's girdle, and passion's bridle." Trench concludes his article by saying that this word "is the habitual inner self-government, with its constant rein on all passions and desires" (Trench, pp. 69-72).

"When we are foolish, we want to conquer the world; when we are wise, we want to conquer self. Our life is measured not by what we win; our life is measured by the thing we strive for" (G. H. Morrison).

This word connotes a "cool head and balanced mind" and has been rendered "keep your head" (Selwyn on 1 Pet. 4:7), "keep your mind steady and clear" or "keep cool" (Wiersbe on 1 Pet. 4:7), be "level-headed" (Adams on 1 Pet. 4:7), "preserve your sanity" (Barclay on 1 Pet. 4:7). It faces things realistically, free from delusion. It describes sound judgment that exercises restraint and is not impulsive. Several ancient secular authors say that it is the opposite of the Greek word from which we get the English word "mania," that is, "frenzy, madness" (Wiersbe on 1 Pet. 4:7; Acts 26:24). It does not allow emotion to take over; it keeps cool under pressure. Balanced thinking, calmness, and self-control are inherent in the word (Adams on 1 Pet. 4:7). It is thinking about and evaluating situations maturely and correctly (Grudem on 1 Pet. 4:7).

William Barclay says that this verb characterizes a man who is pre-eminently sane and adds, "The great characteristic of sanity is that it sees things in their proper proportions; it sees what things are important and what things are not important; it is not swept away by sudden and capricious and transitory enthusiasms; it is prone neither to unbalanced fanaticism nor to unrealizing indifference. It is only when we see the affairs and the activities of earth in the light of eternity that we see them in their proper proportions and their proper importance. It is when God is given His proper place that all things take their proper places" (Barclay on 1 Pet. 4:7).

ILLUSTRATION

We react emotionally. Test pilots have a litmus test for evaluating problems. When something goes wrong, they ask, "Is this thing still flying?" If the answer is yes, there's no immediate danger, no need to overreact. When Apollo 12 took off, the spacecraft was hit by lightning. The entire console began to glow with orange and red trouble lights. There was a temptation to "Do Something!" But the pilots asked themselves, "Is this thing still flying in the right direction?" The answer was yes—it was headed for the moon. They let the lights glow as they addressed the individual problems, and watched orange and red lights blink out, one by one. That's something to think about in any pressure situation. If your thing is still flying, think first, then act (Capt. Alan Bean, USN, Apollo Astronaut, in *Reader's Digest*).

APPLICATION

When we say, "I know I should not _____, but ...." we are not being sensible. Someone has put it like this: "At the banquet, they passed the extra piece of yummy, heavily iced cake to the overweight senior saint. He had already eaten one piece. 'Oh, I shouldn't,' he said. But he did. A young woman who sat watching the senior saint was agonizing over an alcohol addiction. 'I shouldn't,' she echoed later that evening. But she did. A teenager who watched was struggling with his obsession with pornography. 'I shouldn't,' he said that night. But he did. A mother who watched was deliberating whether or not to leave her husband for an attractive man at work. 'I shouldn't,' she said to herself. But she did. A young pastor, wrestling with resentment pushing him toward resigning his church, watched the senior saint succumb to temptation. 'I shouldn't,' he resisted."

I have had people who were deep in credit card debt say to me, "I should get out of debt," but they keep charging. I heard of a man in ICU because of a heart attack, eating a hamburger. Then there was the man who bought tools he did not need and would never use! "It is not so important to be serious as it is to be serious about important things" (Robert M. Hutchins).

PATIENCE

DEFINITION

Another common New Testament word that repeatedly occurs in the New Testament to describe what we should be is the word "patient." The Greek word for "patience" means "long tempered." It is translated "suffers long" (1 Cor. 13:4), "longsuffering" (Gal. 5:22; Eph. 4:2; Col. 1:11; 3:12), "patience" (Heb. 6:12; see 1 Thess. 5:14). It occurs 25 times in the New Testament. Richard Trench says that it is "a long holding out on the mind before it gives room to action or passion—generally to passion." He adds, "Anger usually, but not universally, is the passion thus long held aloof" (Trench, p. 196).

DESCRIPTION

As we have seen, the Greek word for "endurance" means "remaining under, to bear patiently, endure." It is translated "patience" (1 Tim. 6:11; Jas. 1:3), "perseverance" (2 Pet. 1:6; Rom. 5:3), "endurance" (Heb. 12:1). The noun and the verb occur 48 times in the New Testament.

Trench says that the Greek word translated "patience" "expresses patience in respect of persons" and the one rendered "endure" is patience "in respect to things." He goes on to say that when patient people have to deal with injurious people, they do not suffer themselves to be "easily to be provoked by them, or to blaze up into anger." On the other hand, the person who endures is the one "who, under a great siege of trials, bears up, and does not lose heart or courage." He adds that only the first word is an attribute of God (Trench, p. 198).

APPLICATION

Many of us are like Margaret Thatcher, who said, "I am extraordinarily patient, provided I get my own way in the end." Or as Bill Gothard said, "Patience is idling your motor when you feel like stripping a gear." Someone has said,

Patience is a virtue,
Possess it if you can.
Found seldom in a woman,
Never in a man.

God has been patient with us and we should be patient with other people. According to a traditional Hebrew story, Abraham was sitting outside his tent one evening when he saw an old man, weary from age and journey, coming toward him. Abraham rushed out, greeted him, and invited him into his tent. There he washed the old man's feet and gave him food and drink.

The old man immediately began eating without saying any prayer or blessing. So Abraham asked him, "Don't you worship God?"

The old traveler replied, "I worship fire only and reverence no other god."

When he heard this, Abraham became incensed, grabbed the old man by the shoulders, and threw him out his tent into the cold night air.

After the old man had departed, God called to his friend Abraham and asked where the stranger was. Abraham replied, "I forced him out because he did not worship you."

God answered, "I have suffered him these eighty years although he dishonors me. Could you not endure him one night?"

In a message delivered to pastors, Dallas Willard, professor of philosophy at USC pointed out that we go to 1 Corinthians 13 and try to do what it says. First Corinthians 13 does not tell *us* what to do. It tells us what *love* does. If you want the characteristics of 1 Corinthians 13 in your life, be loving.

GRATITUDE

PEOPLE ARE NOT GRATEFUL

In Romans 1, Paul speaks about the fact that God has revealed Himself in creation (Rom. 1:20). He goes on to say, "Because, although they knew God, they did not glorify Him as God, nor were thankful" (Rom. 1:21). The word translated "knew" is the usual Greek word for "know." It can also mean "perceive, understand." In this passage, it is referring to the knowledge of God as revealed in creation (Rom. 1:19-20). The human mind perceives of the notion of God, but that's not the problem. The problem is that having that knowledge, people do not glorify God as God nor are they thankful. Nature reveals God as great and good, but people refuse to recognize Him, worship Him, or be thankful to Him. People are not grateful.

A story is told of a mother and son who lived in a forest. One day when they were out a tornado surprised them. The mother clung to a tree and tried to hold her son. But the swirling winds carried him into the sky. He was gone. The woman began to weep and pray: "Please, O Lord, bring back my boy! He's all I have. I'd do anything not to lose him. If you'll bring him back, I'll serve you all my days." Suddenly the boy toppled from the sky, right at her feet—a bit mussed up, but safe and sound. His mother joyfully brushed him off. Then she stopped for a moment, looked to the sky, and said, "He had a hat, Lord."

GOD WANTS US TO BE GRATEFUL

In Colossians 3, Paul lists virtues that are characteristic of spiritual maturity. He adds, "Let the peace of God rule in your hearts, to which also you were called in one body; and be thankful" (Col. 3:15). The structure of the passage suggests that this imperative is connected with letting the peace of God rule in a person's heart and publicly in the assembly. More specifically, believers are to be thankful that God has called them to peace in one body. Grateful people acknowledge that God is in control of their lives and circumstances and that He orders all things for their welfare. As believers recognize that fact and are thankful for it, peace reigns. Paul earlier prayed that gratitude would be a mark of their lives (Col. 1:12). Here, he exhorts them to thankfulness. The Puritans called the doctrine of sanctification, the doctrine of gratitude.

The ultimate virtue is love (Col. 3:14), but close to the top is gratitude. "A thankful heart is not only the greatest virtue but the parent of all other virtues" (Cicero). We complain when we should be thankful. We see the negative side of life when we should see the positive side of life. Just think about all the things you complain about for which you should be grateful. The list is probably long. This is a list that could have been written by many of us.

I AM THANKFUL FOR …

The partner who hogs the covers every night, because he is not out with someone else.

The child who is not cleaning his room, but is watching TV, because that means he is at home and not on the streets.

For the taxes that I pay, because it means that I am employed.

For the mess to clean after a party because it means that I have been surrounded by friends.

For the clothes that fit a little too snug, because it means I have enough to eat.

For my shadow that watches me work, because it means I am in the sunshine.

For a lawn that needs mowing, windows that need cleaning, and gutters that need fixing, because it means I have a home.

For all the complaints I hear about the government because it means that we have freedom of speech.

For the parking spot I find at the far end of the parking lot, because it means I am capable of walking and that I have been blessed with transportation.

For my huge heating bill, because it means I am warm.

For the lady behind me in church who sings off key, because it means that I can hear.

For the pile of laundry and ironing, because it means I have clothes to wear.

For weariness and aching muscles at the end of the day, because it means I have been capable of working hard.

For the alarm that goes off in the early morning hours, because it means that I am alive.

And finally...For too much e-mail, because it means I have friends who are thinking of me.

SUMMARY

Being spiritually mature includes being sensible, being patient, and being grateful.
Other virtues could be added, such as contentment, forgiveness, tenderheartedness, etc. First Thessalonians is about spiritual maturity and it covers faith, hope, and love. I once saw one-word banners hanging a church. The words were joy, peace, thankfulness, godliness, unity, forgiveness, love,

gentleness, wisdom, hope, generosity, compassion, patience, mutual affection, self-control, and humility. Later I learned that the pastor was preaching a series on each of those words. He called them the fruit of the Spirit.

In the midst of tragedy, we can be grateful. In 1636, during the Thirty Years' War—one of the worst wars in the history of mankind in terms of the sheer number of deaths, epidemics, and the economic results—there was a godly pastor whose name was Martin Rinkert. In a single year, this pastor buried 5,000 people in his parish, about fifteen a day. He lived with the worst that life could do. But if you look in your hymnal, you'll find that in the middle of that time, he wrote a table grace for his children, our Thanksgiving hymn:

> "Now thank we all our God
> With hearts and hands and voices,
> Who wondrous things has done,
> In whom his world rejoices."

We should be grateful even when we are having a difficult time. When he was 7 years of age, his family was forced out of their home, and he went to work. When he was 9, his mother died. He lost his job as a store clerk when he was 20. He wanted to go to law school, but he didn't have the education. At age 23 he went into debt to be a partner in a small store. Three years later the business partner died, and the resulting debt took years to repay.

When he was 28, after courting a girl for four years, he asked her to marry him, and she turned him down. On his third try, he was elected to Congress, at age 37, but failed to be re-elected. His son died at four years of age. When this man was 45, he ran for the Senate and lost. At age 47, he ran for the vice-presidency and lost, but at age 51 he was elected president of the United States.

The man was Abraham Lincoln, the man mentioned in the last chapter as one who learned endurance. He also learned gratitude. It was Abraham Lincoln who established the annual celebration of Thanksgiving in 1863—in the midst of the Civil War. Lincoln learned how important it is to stop and thank God, even in the midst of great difficulties.

Abraham Lincoln was sensible, patient, and started the Thanksgiving holiday. I am not suggesting that we should be like him. He is only an example. We should be like Christ and if we are, we will be sensible, patient, and grateful.

CHAPTER FIVE

THE FOUNDATION OF THE SPIRITUAL LIFE

We have looked at the goal of the spiritual life, but where should we start? The Keswick approach to the spiritual life, which is named after a town in England, begins their weeklong "convention" on the subject of sin. After attending one of those meetings as a young man, an older Christian pointed out that the Scripture does not do that. The Scripture begins with the baptism of the Holy Spirit. It is the foundation of the spiritual life.

Frankly, the baptism of the Holy Spirit can be confusing. When people hear the expression "the baptism of the Holy Spirit," they immediately think of Pentecostalism, which teaches that the baptism is an experience after conversion whereby believers receive the Holy Spirit. Is that what the Bible teaches? Two questions need to be answered concerning the baptism of the Holy Spirit.

WHEN DO BELIEVERS RECEIVE THE BAPTISM?

THE PROMISE
John the Baptist predicted that Jesus would baptize with the Holy Spirit (Mt. 3:11; Mk. 1:8; Lk. 3:16; Jn. 1:33). After the resurrection, Jesus told the disciples to wait in Jerusalem for the baptism of the Holy Spirit (Acts 1:4-5). At this point, the baptism of the Holy Spirit was still future.

THE FULFILLMENT
The baptism of the Holy Spirit began in Acts 2. The expression "the baptism of the Holy Spirit" does not appear in Acts 2. Acts 2 simply says they were "all filled with the Holy Spirit" (Acts 2:4), but what is said later in the book

of Acts indicates this was the beginning of the baptism of Holy Spirit.

While Peter was preaching to the people in Cornelius' house, "the Holy Spirit fell on all those who heard the word" (Acts 10:44). Again, the expression "the baptism of the Holy Spirit" does not appear in Acts 10, but what is said later indicates that is what happened.

When Peter returned to Jerusalem, he explained what happened in Cornelius' house by saying "As I began to speak, the Holy Spirit fell upon them, as upon us at the beginning. Then I remember the word of the Lord, how He said, 'John indeed baptized with water, but you should be baptized with the Holy Spirit'" (Acts 11:15-16). The expression "as upon us at the beginning" can only refer to Acts 2 because in Acts 1 the baptism of the Holy Spirit was still future (Acts 1:5). So these verses in Acts 11 explain that what happened in Acts 2 and Acts 10 was the baptism of the Holy Spirit and that the baptism of the Holy Spirit began on the day of Pentecost in Acts 2.

THE NORM TODAY

The confusion and conflict over the baptism of the Holy Spirit are *when* it takes place today. In Acts 2, people receive the baptism *after* their conversion. In Acts 10, it happened *at* conversion. What is the norm?

In Acts, receiving the Holy Spirit *after* conversion was extremely rare. It was not the norm. In the approximate 30 years covered in the book of Acts, people received the Holy Spirit after conversion only three times (Acts 2, 8, 19). Moreover, the New Testament does not recognize the possibility of being a Christian apart from possession of the Spirit (Jn. 3:5; Acts 11:17; Rom. 8:9; 1 Cor. 12:3; Gal. 3:2; 1 Thess. 1:5ff.; Tit. 3:5; Heb. 6:4; 1 Pet. 1:2; 1 Jn. 3:24; 4:13).

If it was not the norm, why did the baptism of the Holy Spirit happen *after* conversion on three occasions in Acts? The first time the baptism of the Holy Spirit occurred was in Acts 2. Since the baptism of the Holy Spirit first happened to people who were already believers, obviously it had to happen *after* their conversion. In Acts 8, if the Holy Spirit had come on the Samaritans apart from the laying on of hands of Peter and John, there would have forever been two churches because the Jewish Christians and the Samaritan Christians would have had nothing to do with each other. So the baptism of the Holy Spirit came on the Samaritans after their conversion by the laying on of hands to establish unity between the Jewish church in Jerusalem and the Samaritan church in Samaria. In Acts 19, disciples of John the Baptist said they had not heard of the coming of the Holy Spirit. In other words, they missed out on what happened on the day of Pentecost. Prior to the coming of the Holy Spirit on the day of Pentecost, believers were not baptized with the Holy Spirit (Jn.

16:13; Acts 1:5; 2:4; 11:15-16; 1 Cor. 12:13). So in that case, they received the baptism of the Holy Spirit after their conversion.

In the case of Acts 19, there was another factor. Part of the purpose of the latter part of a book of Acts is to demonstrate the authority of the apostle Paul. Paul was able to do all that Peter did. Hence, in Acts 19, Paul was able to lay hands on the believers who were converted in the ministry of John the Baptist before Pentecost so that he could do what Peter did in Acts 8.

Therefore, except for a few special occasions, which occurred for special reasons, after Pentecost, every believer receives the baptism of the Holy Spirit at conversion (1 Cor. 12:13). Contrary to the Pentecostal movement, the baptism of the Holy Spirit is not a work of the Holy Spirit subsequent to salvation. All believers are baptized into the body of Christ at conversion (Rom. 8:9; Eph. 1:3; Col. 2:10). There are no commands or conditions for the baptism of the Holy Spirit. Furthermore, the one person in the New Testament who wanted to seek something connected with the Holy Spirit was rebuked sharply (Acts 8:18-24).

By the way, that means that since the baptism of the Holy Spirit began on the day of Pentecost and it places believers in the body of Christ, which is the church (Eph. 1:22-23), the church began on the day of Pentecost.

WHAT IS THE SIGNIFICANCE?

Six verses in the epistles refer to the baptism of the Holy Spirit (Rom. 6:3; 1 Cor. 12:13; Gal. 3:27; Eph. 4:5; Col. 2:12; 1 Pet. 3:21). The only passage that gives a detailed explanation is Romans 6. In the most detailed discussion of the spiritual life in the New Testament (Rom. 6-8), Paul begins with the baptism of the Holy Spirit (Rom. 6:1-14). It is the foundation of the spiritual life. There are three imperatives in Romans 6:1-14.

KNOW
The first command in Romans 6:1-14 is "know" (Rom. 6:3, 6). Believers need to know several things.

> 1. Believers need to know that they were baptized into Christ. Paul says, "Or did you not know that as many of us as were baptized into Christ Jesus were baptized into His death?" (Rom. 6:3). Simply put, believers were united to Christ (Rom. 6:5). When I got married, I was united to Patricia. We became one.

2. Believers need to know that they were baptized into Christ's death. Paul says, "We were buried with Him through baptism into death" (Rom. 6:4; see also 6:3, 5-6). What does that mean? Something died. What died? Paul says the old man died (Rom. 6:6). The expression "old man" has been interpreted to mean the believer's sinful nature as if it were some part inside believers that died.

An old deacon who frequently led the prayer meetings would often conclude his petitions with the words, "O Lord, clean all the cobwebs out of my life!" Finally, a man who lived next door to him could stand it no longer, for he knew that he was a self-seeking, carnal Christian. So one Wednesday night when the old fellow ended in his usual manner, his neighbor jumped to his feet and shouted, "Don't do it, Lord! Don't do it! Make him kill the spider!" Some think of the old man as a spider that can be killed. I wish it were that easy.

The word "man" does not refer to just *part* of a person. The "old man" is the *whole man* who lived before conversion. The old man is the man of old who existed before the believer came to Christ. This person was crucified with Christ. He no longer exists. Simply put, believers in Jesus Christ are not the same people they were before conversion. When I got married, I was united to Patricia. The old Mike, *the single Mike* died. He no longer exists. He is dead to blondes, brunettes, and redheads.

God had two purposes in mind in crucifying the old man (see the two clauses which begin with "that" in Rom. 6:6). First, the old man was crucified "that the body of sin might be done away with" (Rom. 6:6). Colossians 2:11, a parallel passage to this one, indicates that the body of sin is used figuratively of the mass of sin. This mass of sin was abolished when the old man was crucified with Christ.

The second purpose was "that we should no longer be slaves to sin" (Rom. 6:6). The old man, who was a slave to sin, was crucified. The believer is now a new person, who does not have to be a slave to sin. Believers *should* no longer be slaves, but if they do not follow Paul's instructions in this passage, they *could* be (Rom. 7:23).

Paul explains ("for"): "For he who has died has been freed from sin" (Rom. 6:7). The word translated "freed" is the Greek word "justification," which is a forensic term. In a figurative sense, the word means "freed." The idea is that the believer no longer has any legal obligation to sin. Sin lost its case in court. The illustration comes from slavery. A slave owner has legal claims over a slave. The slave is legally obligated to obey, but if the slave is dead, he is freed from that obligation. If the slave owner were to order the slave to lie or kill, the slave would have to say "My tongue and my hands no longer obey me *as a slave.*"

3. Believers need to know that they were baptized into Christ's resurrection (Rom. 6:4-5). Spiritually, believers are raised to walk a new kind of life (Rom. 6:4). They are alive to God (Rom. 6:11). When I got married, I began a new kind of life, married life.

4. Believers need to know that they were baptized into Christ's body (1 Cor. 12:13). When I got married, I was united to Patricia's family. You don't marry a person; you marry a family.

The point of Romans 6 is that believers do not have to sin (Rom. 6:2, 6, 7). Believers can live a new kind of life with Christ (Rom. 6:4, 8). Believers may sin, but they do not have to; they can choose not to sin. A prisoner has to obey the warden, but when he is pardoned and set free, he is no longer obligated to obey what the warden commands prisoners to do. Believers in Jesus Christ have been freed from sin. They are no longer obligated to obey the impulses of the flesh.

BELIEVE

The second command in Romans 6:1-4 is believe. "Now if we died with Christ we believe that we shall also live with Him, knowing that Christ having been raised from the dead, dies no more. Death no longer has dominion over Him" (Rom. 6:8-9). Paul's explanation (see "for" in 6:10) is that Christ died *once* and He now lives unto God (Rom. 6:10). He says, "Likewise you also reckon yourselves to be dead indeed to sin, but alive to God in Christ Jesus our Lord" (Rom. 6:11). "Reckon" is an accounting term which means "to take into account, calculate." In this passage, it is virtually equivalent to "believe." It is one thing to know that you are dead to sin; it is another to believe it. It is one thing to know the governor has pardoned you and you are no longer a prisoner; it is another to accept that as true.

If you reckon wrong, you will make a mistake. I reckoned that I had $159 in my checking account when I only had $59. Thankfully, when I paid a $61 parking ticket, my overdraft protection prevented a bounced check.

The concept of Romans 6:8-11 is similar to, if not the same as, the modern concept of "self-image." If we believe that we are dead, we will act accordingly. At conversion, God makes us new. We must reckon by faith that we are indeed new creatures in Christ. Sin no longer is to be the center of our lives. Christ is to be the focus.

A number of women who had facial defects of one kind or another went to a plastic surgeon requesting that the defect be corrected so that they could be beautiful. He performed plastic surgery on all of them. To his surprise, some of them concluded that the defect was corrected and, therefore, they were beautiful. Others, however, responded to the surgery by saying they were still ugly. The plastic surgeon said that the difference was not the fact of their facial features, but of their self-image. Those who believed that they were beautiful concluded they were beautiful. Those who believed they were ugly concluded they were ugly. The surgeon ultimately wrote a book entitled *Psycho-cybernetics*. His name was Maxwell Maltz.

In a similar fashion, believers need to reckon on the fact that radical surgery has been done. They are now new creatures in Christ and are capable of righteous living. This is not to say that they are no longer capable of sin. As Paul will explain later, they still have the flesh and are very much capable of sin. However, their basic nature is that they are now new creatures in Christ. Some teach that Christians are saved sinners, that is, their basic nature is that they are sinners and they happen to be saved. The New Testament teaches that we are saints who happen to still have the flesh.

The Puritan theologian John Owen once wrote that his biggest challenge as a pastor was persuading non-Christians that they were slaves to sin and Christians that they were dead to sin. We need to undergo a paradigm shift in our thinking, to see ourselves differently, as those introduced to a new way of living.

OBEY

The third command in Romans 6:1-14 is obedience. Paul writes, "Therefore do not let sin reign in your mortal body, that you should obey it in its lusts, and do not present your members to sin, but present yourselves to God as being alive from the dead, and your members as instruments of righteousness to God" (Rom. 6:12-13).

The believer, being in Christ, is dead to sin. As every believer knows, sin is still a problem. The sin principle is still present and can express itself through "the mortal body," that is, the body destined to death, but sin has no right to reign; therefore Paul says, do not obey sin, but God. Don't use any member of your body to sin; use the members of your body, like your legs, arms, and mouth as instruments of righteousness unto God. Don't use your hands to steal or your mouth to lie. Use your hands to help others and your mouth to praise God. In short, obey the Lord. You have a choice.

SUMMARY

The foundation of the spiritual life is the baptism of the Holy Spirit, which all believers receive at conversion, uniting them to Christ and one another.
Perception of self determines personal behavior. Years ago William R. Newell, the famous Bible teacher, was conducting a conference in China for the China Inland Mission. As he left, he said to a mission leader, "Pray for me that I shall be nothing!" With a twinkle in his eye, the director responded, "Newell, you are nothing! Take it by faith!" (R. Kent Hughes, *Acts: The Church Afire*, p. 27). Granted, Jesus said that without Him we could do nothing (Jn. 15:5); that does not mean we are nothing. We are in Christ and His body. That is far from nothing. You need to believe who you are in Christ.

A friend of mine told of stopping at a stop sign and being hit by the car behind him, which did not stop. There was no great damage done to life or limb or either car, but my friend's first response was anger because this accident was going to make him late for an appointment. Before he got out of the car, he said to himself, "I do not have to be angry. I am a believer in Christ who can be kind. I believe that and I choose to on this occasion do that." He then got out of the car and was kind to an embarrassed motorist.

The critical issue is that we understand that as believers in Christ we are new creatures. We must reckon on that new position and act accordingly.

I think it was J. Vernon McGee who put it like this: In your mind, go back in time about 150 years to the days before the Civil War. Imagine you are visiting one of the great cities of the South like Savannah, Atlanta, Birmingham, Jackson, or New Orleans. As you approach the center of town you hear a commotion as a crowd gathers for a public auction and you gather round to watch the proceedings. The first thing you notice in the crowd is an uncouth, foulmouthed, loud, boisterous man who you know, by reputation only, as the meanest, cruelest, most hateful man around. You also notice in the crowd another man who stands out for his dignity, genteel mannerisms and soft-spoken tone, and recognize him also by reputation as a most kind, gentle, and gracious man. Both men, along with the crowd, wait for the auction to begin.

Then you see an auctioneer step to the podium and a beautiful, young, black girl, about 20 years of age, who is about to sold in an auction block. The girls dress is old and worn, but clean. She is obviously filled with fear as the bidding begins.

From the outset, the loud obnoxious man seemed to have his evil eyes set on this lovely innocent young lady. She obviously knew of his reputation and cringed in fear as he opened the bidding. When the kind gentleman saw her fear, he too placed a bid. Soon only these two men were involved in a bidding war as the price of the girl rose higher and higher. Finally, the evil man bowed out of the bidding when he realized that the price of the girl was more than he was willing to pay.

When the auctioneer closed the bidding, the kind gentleman paid the price for his purchase, was handed the Bill-of-Sale, and turned to leave. The young girl started to follow her new master. He turned to her and asked, "Where are you going?" "Why I'm going with you," she responded; "You bought me and I belong to you." "O! You misunderstood," the man said, "I didn't buy you to make you my slave, I bought you to set you free." Then he took the Bill-of-Sale and wrote across in big block letters – FREE! – signed his name and gave it to the girl. "I don't understand," the girl said. "You mean I am free." "Yes, you are free." "I can go wherever I want and do as I please." "Exactly, You are free." "Mister, I don't know who you are, but no one has ever shown such love and kindness to me. If I am free to do as I please, nothing would please me more than to go with you and serve you till the day I die."

That day she went home with Abraham Lincoln, not as his slave, but as his willing servant. The story may be true, but I suspect it is an allegory. Whether it is true or not, it illustrates that we are no longer slaves, we are free to obey our new master.

CHAPTER SIX

THE PATTERN OF THE SPIRITUAL LIFE

Trying to figure out what the spiritual life is about can be confusing. It is particularly puzzling if you listen to preachers. Many want to make the critical issue a crisis experience, such as dedication, rededication, full surrender, etc. As a young Christian, that bothered me. So I decided to see what the Bible says. I quickly discovered that turning to the Bible can also be baffling. The gospels talk about being a disciple. But after the book of Acts, the word "disciple" never appears again in the New Testament. The book of Acts speaks about being "filled with the Spirit," but that phrase rarely occurs outside of the writings of Luke. Paul uses various terms such as "present your body" and "walk." Peter exhorts, "grow in grace." John commands, "Confess your sins." My question was, "Why don't the epistles agree?"

What do all of these terms mean? Do they mean the same thing? Surely, these various concepts are complementary and not contradictory. What is the *pattern* of the spiritual life in the New Testament? Is there a blueprint in the Bible for the spiritual life? The answer is "yes."

THE PATTERN

Paul says, "And do not present your members *as* instruments of unrighteousness to sin, but present yourselves to God as being alive from the dead, and your members *as* instruments of righteousness to God" (Rom. 6:13). In Romans 6, Paul teaches that all believers have been united to Jesus Christ. Believers are "legally" dead to sin and alive to God. The problem is that although we are legally dead to sin, we still sin. Therefore, Paul takes the spiritual life to the next level. For what has happened to us to be a practical reality, we must not use the members of our body to sin, but we must use them as instruments of righteousness. That is the pattern of the spiritual life. It is negative and positive. Stop this; start that. Do not do this; do that.

That pattern is repeated throughout the New Testament. It can be plainly seen in Ephesians and Colossians, where Paul uses the figures of speech of "put off" and "put on," but it also appears one way or another in every book in the New Testament. Let's start with Ephesians.

In Ephesians, Paul says, "That you put off concerning your former conduct, the old man which grows corrupt according to the deceitful lusts" (Eph. 4:22). "Put off" was used of removing a garment, like taking off a coat. It is being used here figuratively of removing, renouncing, stopping something. "Put away," Paul says, "your former way of living," here called the old man.

Many have suggested that the grave clothes of Lazarus are a picture of what Paul is teaching. When Lazarus died, he was wrapped in grave clothes and laid in a tomb. Christ cried, "Lazarus, come forth!" John then says, "And he who had died came out bound hand and foot with grave clothes, and his face was wrapped with a cloth" (Jn. 11:44). Imagine! He was alive but still bound with grave clothes. These needed to be removed so he could be totally free. Likewise, Paul is saying, "You are alive to God, so put off the grave clothes of the old life."

Paul adds, "And that you put on the new man which was created according to God, in righteousness and true holiness" (Eph. 4:24). "Put on," like "put off" (Eph. 4:22), was used of clothing oneself. Here it is being used figuratively of the new spiritual self that needs to be constantly adorned with spiritual virtues.

That is only the beginning. Consider the rest of the New Testament, especially the epistles from Romans to Revelation.

Matthew 16:24: "Then Jesus said to His disciples, "If anyone desires to come after Me, let him deny himself, and take up his cross, and follow Me'" (Mt. 16:24; see also Mk. 8:23; Lk. 9:23; and purging and abiding in Jn. 15:2-4).

Romans 12:1-2: "I beseech you therefore, brethren, by the mercies of God, that you present your bodies a living sacrifice, holy, acceptable to God, *which is* your reasonable service. And do not be conformed to this world, but be transformed by the renewing of your mind, that you may prove what *is* that good and acceptable and perfect will of God."

Romans 13:12-14: "The night is far spent, the day is at hand. Therefore let us cast off the works of darkness, and let us put on the armor of light. Let us walk properly, as in the day, not in revelry and drunkenness, not in lewdness and lust, not in strife and envy. But put on the Lord Jesus Christ, and make no provision for the flesh, to *fulfill its* lusts." The Greek word translated "cast off" is the same translate "put off" in Ephesians 4:22 and the one translated "put on" in Romans 13:12 and 13 is the same one translated "put on" in Ephesians 4:24.

1 Corinthians 6:18-20: "Flee sexual immorality. Every sin that a man does is outside the body, but he who commits sexual immorality sins against his own body. Or do you not know that your body is the temple of the Holy Spirit *who is* in you, whom you have from God, and you are not your own? For you were bought at a price; therefore glorify God in your body and in your spirit, which are God's."

2 Corinthians 7:1: "Therefore, having these promises, beloved, let us cleanse ourselves from all filthiness of the flesh and spirit, perfecting holiness in the fear of God."

Galatians 5:19 and 22: Paul speaks of the "works of the flesh" (Gal. 5:19) and the "fruit of the Spirit" (Gal. 5:23).

Colossians 3:3-4 speaks of being spiritually dead and alive, of having put off the old man (Col. 3:9) and having put on the new man (Col. 3:10). Paul says, "But now you yourselves are to put off all these: anger, wrath, malice, blasphemy, filthy language out of your mouth" (Col. 3:8). The Greek word translated "put off" is the same one used in Ephesians 4:22. Paul lists five vices that are to be taken off like a coat. Then he adds, "Therefore, as *the* elect of God, holy and beloved, put on tender mercies, kindness, humility, meekness, longsuffering" (Col 3:12). The Greek word translated "put on" is the same one used in Ephesians 4:24. Paul lists five virtues that are to be put on like a coat.

Philippians 2:14-15: "Do all things without complaining and disputing that you may become blameless and harmless, children of God without fault in the midst of a crooked and perverse generation, among whom you shine as lights in the world."

First Thessalonians 5:6-8: "Therefore let us not sleep, as others *do,* but let us watch and be sober. For those who sleep, sleep at night, and those who get drunk are drunk at night. But let us who are of the day be sober, putting on the breastplate of faith and love, and *as* a helmet the hope of salvation."

Second Thessalonians 3:6-7: "But we command you, brethren, in the name of our Lord Jesus Christ, that you withdraw from every brother who walks disorderly and not according to the tradition which he received from us. For you yourselves know how you ought to follow us, for we were not disorderly among you."

First Timothy 6:11: "But you, O man of God, flee these things and pursue righteousness, godliness, faith, love, patience, gentleness." In the Pastoral Epistles, 1 and 2 Timothy, Paul uses flee/pursue instead of put off/put on.

Second Timothy 2:22: "Flee also youthful lusts; but pursue righteousness, faith, love, peace with those who call on the Lord out of a pure heart."

Titus 2:12: "Teaching us that, denying ungodliness and worldly lusts, we should live soberly, righteously, and godly in the present age."

Philemon: 16 "No longer as a slave but more than a slave; a beloved brother, especially to me but how much more to you, both in the flesh and in the Lord."

Hebrews 12:1: "Therefore we also, since we are surrounded by so great a cloud of witnesses, let us lay aside every weight, and the sin which so easily ensnares *us,* and let us run with endurance the race that is set before us." The Greek word translated "lay aside" is the same one translated "put off" in Ephesians 4:22.

James 1:21: "Therefore lay aside all filthiness and overflow of wickedness, and receive with meekness the implanted word, which is able to save your souls." The Greek word translated "lay aside" is the same one translated "put off" in Ephesians 4:22.

First Peter 2:1-2: "Therefore, laying aside all malice, all deceit, hypocrisy, envy, and all evil speaking as newborn babes, desire the pure milk of the word, that you may grow thereby." The Greek word translated "laying aside" is the same one translated "put off" in Ephesians 4:22.

Second Peter 3:17-18: "You therefore, beloved, since you know *this* beforehand, beware lest you also fall from your own steadfastness, being led away with the error of the wicked, but grow in the grace and knowledge of our Lord and Savior Jesus Christ. To Him *be* the glory both now and forever. Amen."

First John 1:9 and 2:3: "If we confess our sins, He is faithful and just to forgive us *our* sins and to cleanse us from all unrighteousness" and "Now by this we know that we know Him, if we keep His commandments."

Second John 8: "Look to yourselves, that we do not lose those things we worked for, but *that* we may receive a full reward."

Third John 11: "Beloved, do not imitate what is evil, but what is good. He who does good is of God, but he who does evil has not seen God."

Jude 17 and 21: "Remember" (mockers) and "keep yourself in the love of God."

Revelation 3:19-20: "As many as I love, I rebuke and chasten. Therefore be zealous and repent. Behold, I stand at the door and knock. If anyone hears My voice and opens the door, I will come in to him and dine with him, and he with Me."

These verses cover every book in the New Testament. All the authors in the New Testament agree on the basic pattern of the spiritual life. It is both negative and positive. Paul, James, Peter and the writer to the Hebrews even use the same Greek word ("put off")!

The same pattern is in the Old Testament. Psalm 1:1-2: "Blessed *is* the man Who walks not in the counsel of the ungodly, Nor stands in the path of sinners, Nor sits in the seat of the scornful. But his delight *is* in the law of the LORD, And in His law he meditates day and night."

The pattern of the spiritual life is to put off vices and put on virtues. It is vital that *both of these be done.* To put off a vice and not put on the corresponding virtue is to leave oneself naked and vulnerable. It is only half the job. Yet that is what many believers do and churches practice. For example, when dealing with alcoholics, we aim at getting them to stay sober. That's good, but that is only half the job. The goal of spiritual life is Christ-like maturity, which is way beyond staying sober. On the other hand, to put on virtues and not put off vices is to cover the vices.

THE PRINCIPLE

Embedded in the pattern is a principle. Think about the image. If you put off and put on, you are replacing one piece of clothing with another. This is the principle of replacement.

REPLACE STEALING WITH GIVING

Paul says, "Let him who stole steal no longer, but rather let him labor, working with his hands, what is good, that he may have something to give him who has need" (Eph. 4:28). Stealing is to be replaced with giving. If we steal, we hurt others, so we are to work to be able to help others. Stealing is using another's labor to satisfy one's own desires. Working is using one's own labor to supply another's need.

REPLACE BAD SPEECH WITH GOOD SPEECH

Paul exhorts, "Let no corrupt communication proceed out of your mouth, but what is good for necessary edification that it may impart grace to the hearers" (Eph. 4:29). Corrupt communication is to be replaced with "good" communication. The Greek word translated "corrupt" means "bad, worthless, rotten." Figuratively, as it is used here, it means "offensive and injurious." The Greek word translated "edification" means to "build up." What comes out of the believer's mouth should be good, not bad; wholesome, not worthless; redemptive, not rotten. Speech that tears down is to be replaced with speech that builds up.

REPLACE VICES WITH VIRTUES
Paul commands, "Let all bitterness, wrath, anger, clamor, and evil speaking be put away from you, with all malice. And be kind to one another, tenderhearted, forgiving one another, just as God in Christ also forgave you" (Eph. 4:31-32). The Greek word translated "put away" is not the same Greek word that is translated "put off" in verse 22. Sinful vices are to be replaced with godly virtues. Bitterness, wrath, anger, clamor, and evil speaking are to be replaced with kindness, tenderheartedness (compassion) and forgiveness. Don't be hard-hearted (bitter); be tenderhearted.

The principle of replacement is stated simply in Romans 12, "overcome evil with good" (Rom. 12:21).

We are to replace sinful actions, speech and attitudes with godly actions, speech and attitudes. Behavioral and attitudinal changes are needed. Often believers drop sinful habits first. Then, they deal with bad speech and after that, negative attitudes.

THE PROCESS

THE PROBLEM
This pattern and the principle embedded in it seems to suggest that this is to be done instantaneously. Remember Superman? Every time Clark Kent transformed himself into Superman, he went into a telephone booth and stripped off his ordinary business suit. Underneath his ordinary clothes was his official Superman outfit. When he came out of the phone booth in his Superman suit, he could do supernatural things. The impression the metaphor of put off/put on gives is that we can change clothes in an instant and do supernatural things.

What is wrong with that? Can God not change people instantaneously? Does God not change people miraculously?

THE SOLUTION
God can and does change people instantaneously. That often happens to people when they are converted, but within the spiritual life, God does not always work that way. Implied in the put off/put on pattern is progress. The New Testament is abundantly clear that the pattern involves progression. In other words, believers are to grow.

Peter says, "Therefore, laying aside all malice, all deceit, hypocrisy, envy, and all evil speaking, as newborn babes, desire the pure milk of the word, that you may grow thereby" (1 Pet 2:1-2). Remember the Greek word translated "laying aside" is the Greek word for "put off." This is the pattern for the spiritual life. Notice, however, Peter acknowledges that growth is involved. Growth takes time.

Peter says something similar in his second epistle. In chapter 3, he uses the standard pattern for the spiritual life (2 Pet. 3:17-18) and in the process says "grow in the grace and knowledge of our Lord and Savior Jesus Christ" (2 Pet. 3:18; see also Eph. 4:15).

Put off and put on may sound as if the process is instantaneous, but the New Testament recognizes that there is a growth process. It is like wine. Wine takes time. On one occasion, however, Jesus instantaneously changed water into wine, but normally that is not the way God makes wine.

To say the same thing another way, maturity does not happen all at once; it is little by little. In Abraham's day, the land we call "Palestine" was occupied with several nations. God's judgment on those nations was that they would be removed (Gen. 15:16). God promised the land to the Israelites, but He did not give it to them all at once. He gave it to them "little by little." The Old Testament records, "And the LORD your God will drive out those nations before you little by little; you will be unable to destroy them at once, lest the beasts of the field become *too* numerous for you" (Deut 7:22). "And I will send hornets before you, which shall drive out the Hivite, the Canaanite, and the Hittite from before you. I will not drive them out from before you in one year, lest the land become desolate and the beasts of the field become too numerous for you. Little by little I will drive them out from before you until you have increased, and you inherit the land" (Ex. 23:28-30). Likewise, God does not give us spiritual maturity all at once; it is little by little, which means it takes time—a lifetime.

In *The Last Days* Newsletter, Leonard Ravenhill tells about a group of tourists visiting a picturesque village who walked by an old man sitting beside a fence. In a rather patronizing way, one tourist asked, "Were any great men born in this village?" The old man replied, "Nope, only babies." There are no instant spiritually mature believers. Maturity requires growth and growth takes time.

SUMMARY

The pattern of a biblical spiritual life is growth; that is, replacing vices with Christ-like virtues.

The key to the spiritual life is not dedication/consecration/surrender. It is a process. It is a process of growth. At the same time, there is a sense that in order to grow, you must be *committed to the process of growing in your relationship with the Lord*. The Greek word translated "disciple" means "learner." Jesus taught that in order to learn, believers had to be committed to putting Him above all else to follow Him and learn from Him. He said, "If anyone desires to come after Me, let him deny himself, and take up his cross daily, and follow Me" (Lk. 9:23; 14:26-33). The key to marriage is not the wedding ceremony. It is a commitment to the life-long process of developing the relationship with your mate.

To grow, you must make up your mind to grow. William Law says, "If you stop and ask yourself why you are not so devoted as the (early) Christians, your own heart will tell you that it is neither through ignorance nor inability, but purely because you never thoroughly intended it." Dr. Ari Kiev of Cornell University observed that from the moment people decided to concentrate all their energies on a specific objective, they began to surmount the most difficult odds. He concluded, "The establishment of a goal is the key to successful living" (Cornell, *Today in the Word*, July 1990, p. 14).

Set your sights on being Christ-like. If you don't, you will not make it by accident. If you do, by God's grace, you can grow toward Christ-like maturity.

Roger Staubach, former quarterback for the Dallas Cowboys, was a plebe in his first summer at the U.S. Naval Academy and expected to be unobtrusive in the presence of upperclassmen. At breakfast one Sunday, however, an upperclassman began prodding Roger. He was backup quarterback on the football team and was well aware that soon Roger would be in competition with him. "Hey, Staubach!" he barked. "I hear you're going to take my job away. Is that right?"

"No, sir," replied Roger.

The upperclassman pressed the issue. "That's strange," he said. "I'm sure that's what I heard."

"What is your job, sir?" asked Roger.

"Number two quarterback," the upperclassman announced.

"I'm not going to take your job away, sir," Roger assured him.

The upperclassman seemed satisfied until Roger added, "It's the starting-quarterback job that I'm going to take, sir."

And he did (source unknown).

CHAPTER SEVEN

THE REQUIREMENTS OF THE SPIRITUAL LIFE

One of the major words used in the New Testament to describe the spiritual life is "disciple." That is a common concept, but there is conflict and confusion over what is involved. Some say that being a Christian and being a disciple are synonymous. Others contend those are two different things. There is confusion over the requirement for being a disciple. What is a disciple? What are the requirements to be a disciple? In order to answer these questions, consider the use of the word disciple in the Gospels and in Acts and the concept of discipleship in the epistles.

IN THE GOSPELS

THE MEANING
The Greek word translated "disciple" means "learner, pupil." It presumes a teacher. In secular Greek, "disciple" was the usual word for apprentice. Plato called the man learning to play the flute a disciple. The doctor in training under an experienced physician was a disciple (*TDNT*, vol. 4, p. 416). A disciple was an apprentice in a trade, a student of medicine, or a member of a philosophical school (Brown, vol. 1, p. 484). In the Gospels, the word "disciple" is used of being a learner of several different teachers. The Gospels speak of being a disciple of Moses (Jn. 9:28), a disciple of the Pharisees (Mt. 22:15-16; Mk. 2:18; Lk. 5:33), a disciple of John the Baptist (Mt. 9:14; Mk. 2:18; Lk. 5:33; 7:18; Jn. 3:22), and, of course, a disciple of Jesus.

When used to designate a disciple of Jesus, the term "disciple" has a wide variety of meanings. For example, it is used in the general sense of anyone who learned from Jesus (Mt. 8:21; Lk. 6:17; Jn. 4:1). Apparently, some of these "learners" were not saved (Jn. 6:60-66, esp. 64; in Jn. 12:4, Judas is called a disciple). They came to learn from Jesus, but they did not trust in Jesus for the gift of eternal life. The most common meaning of the term "disciple" is a designation of the twelve apostles (Mt. 10:1; 20:17; Lk. 9:1). Gene Getz says that in the four Gospels, it is used more than 80% of the time of one or more of the twelve apostles (Getz, p. 348). The twelve forsook their occupations to travel with and learn from Jesus (Mt. 4:18-22). The twelve became the eleven (Mt. 28:16). One of the *twelve* was not saved (Jn. 17:12)!

Thus, a disciple in the Gospels was anyone from a learner, who did not trust Jesus for eternal life, to a constant companion who traveled with Him, but not even all those who traveled with Him trusted Him for eternal life. So, who is a true disciple of Jesus?

REQUIREMENTS
During His ministry, Jesus gave His disciples the requirements for being a real disciple, one who *really* learns. After His resurrection, Jesus mentioned a requirement He had not stated during His ministry. Here is what is necessary to be a disciple of Jesus Christ.

1. Depend on Christ for eternal life
To be a disciple one must trust Jesus for eternal life. John records, "As He spoke these words, many believed in Him. Then Jesus said to those Jews who believed Him, 'If you abide in My word, you are My disciples indeed'" (Jn. 8:30-31). Jesus spoke to those *who had believed*, that is, those who had trusted Him for the gift of eternal life. That means they were born again (Jn. 3:1-15); they were possessors of spiritual life (Jn. 10:10). He told those believers that if they were to abide in His Word, they would be disciples indeed. The Greek word translated "indeed" means, "truly." In other words, Jesus spoke to those who *believed* about being a *true* disciple. There is a difference between being a believer and being a disciple. Eternal life is a gift (Jn. 4:10; Eph. 2:8-9; Rom. 3:24); discipleship is costly (Lk. 14:28).

2. Decide to get baptized
To be a disciple, one must be baptized. Before ascending, Jesus gave the Great Commission. The commission is to make disciples (Mt. 28:19). He described a three-step process to do that, namely, going, baptizing, and teaching. Going includes introducing people to Christ (Mk. 16:15-16). Baptizing identifies a believer with a body of believers. Teaching is, of course, instruction. Thus, the Great Commission indicates that baptism, as well as salvation and instruction,

are necessary for being a disciple.

3. Deeply desire to be like Him

To be a disciple one must desire to be a disciple. Jesus said, "If anyone desires to come after me" (Mt. 16:24; Mk. 8:24; Lk. 9:23). Although not generally listed as one of the requirements for discipleship, "desire" is at least a prerequisite, if not a requirement, for following Jesus.

4. Deny yourself as the authority in life

To be a disciple, one must deny himself. Jesus said, "If anyone desires to come after Me, let him deny himself" (Mt. 16:24; Mk. 8:24; Lk. 9:23). The Greek word translated "deny" means "to refuse to recognize, to ignore." To deny oneself is more than self-denial; it is the denial of self. Self-denial is denying oneself a hot fudge sundae; denying oneself is denying the self as the authority in life and making Jesus the supreme authority.

Jesus said, "If anyone comes to Me and does not hate his father and mother, wife and children, brothers and sisters, yes, and his own life also, he cannot be My disciple" (Lk. 14:26). Here, hating is loving less. Genesis 29:30 says that Jacob "loved Rachel more than Leah." The next verse says, "When the LORD saw that Leah was hated" (Gen. 29:31 KJV, which is a literal translation of the Hebrew text). Thus, in the Bible, one sense of the word "hate" is to love less. When Jesus used the word "hate" in Luke 14, He meant loving less. He said so! Matthew's account says, "He who loves father or mother more than Me is not worthy of Me. And he who loves son or daughter more than Me is not worthy of Me" (Mt. 10:37). To be a disciple, one must love the Lord supremely, so much so that all other loves are hatred by comparison. In the final analysis, this is nothing more than the first commandment in the Ten Commandments, namely, "You shall have no other gods before Me" (Ex. 20:3).

To be a disciple, Jesus must be the most important relationship in your life. He must be the supreme authority. Instead of living a self-centered life, being a disciple is living a Christ-centered life.

5. Daily do God's will

To be a disciple, one must take up his cross. Jesus said, "If anyone desires to come after Me, let him deny himself, and take up his cross" (Mt. 16:24; Mk. 8:24; Lk. 9:23; 14:23; Mt. 10:38). Luke's account adds the word daily (Lk. 9:23).

Various explanations have been given of taking up the cross. Some have said it is actually martyrdom (*The Interpreters Bible*). Most who take it literally say it means to be *willing* to be a martyr (Tasker; F. F. Bruce). The problem with that interpretation in Jesus says "take up" the cross, which is an act that takes place *before* dying, and He follows that with "follow Me," which means the person has not died yet. Furthermore, it is be done daily (Lk. 9:23). By far the most common interpretation is that it is a figure for suffering, pain, persecution, shame, humiliation, or rejection (Luther; Calvin; Bonhoeffer; Lenski). Another possibility is that it is submission to the Lord's rule (Michael P. Green, "The Meaning of Cross Bearing," *Bibliotheca Sacra* 140:558, April 1983, pp. 117-127). Green concedes, "Proponents of the submission view are practically nonexistent" (Green, p. 122). He claims Pentecost supports his conclusion. "The only obedience proponent found by this student is J. D. Pentecost. He writes, 'An individual's cross is the revealed will of God for him' (Pentecost, *The Words and Works of Jesus Christ* [Grand Rapids: Zondervan Publishing House, 1981], p. 196) and to take up one's cross is to 'accept God's will for his life (ibid., p. 272)'" (Green, p. 122).

This view fits the context of Matthew 16. Jesus told the disciples He must go to Jerusalem and be killed and be raised the third day (Mt. 16:21). It was then that He told the disciples, "If anyone desires to *come after Me*, let him deny himself and take up *his* cross and follow me" (Mt 16: 24, italics added). In other words, the cross was the will of God for Him. Those who follow Him must take up their cross, the will of God for them.

6. Diligently follow

To be a disciple one must diligently follow Jesus. Jesus said, "If anyone desires to come after Me, let him deny himself, and take up his cross, and follow Me" (Mt. 16:24; Mk. 8:24; Lk. 9:23). When Christ said, "Follow Me," He, no doubt, meant for them to literally forsake everything and travel with Him (Lk. 14:33).

To follow someone presupposes two things: faith and obedience. Remember playing the game "follow the leader" when you were a child? You had to trust the leader and obey every command the leader gave. Jesus said, "If you abide in My word, you are My disciples indeed" (Jn. 8:30-31). Being a disciple means abiding in the Word; that is being obedient to the Word. The one command above all others that a disciple is to keep is the new commandment to love one another (Jn. 13:34). By loving each other, all will know that they were Christ's disciples (Jn. 13:35).

METHOD

In the Gospels, the method of being a disciple was to follow Jesus literally, that is, be physically present with Him. Jesus said, "Follow Me, and I will make you become fishers of men. They immediately left their nets and followed Him" (Mk. 1:17-18). Jesus "appointed twelve, that they might be with Him" (Mk. 3:14). That is why disciples had to leave their families and possessions (Lk. 14:26, 33).

THE RESULT

The result of learning from Jesus was growing to be more and more like Him. There are levels of discipleship, indicating a growth process. Jesus speaks of going from no fruit (Jn. 15:2) to some fruit (Jn. 15:2) to much fruit (Jn. 15:5). Jesus says, "By this, My Father is glorified, that you bear much fruit; so you will be My disciples" (Jn. 15:8). Believers are *really* disciples when they bear *much* fruit.

The ultimate goal is to be like Jesus. As Jesus Himself explained, "A disciple is not above his teacher, but everyone who is perfectly trained will be like his teacher" (Lk. 6:40). To be a disciple one must be a fisher of men. When Jesus first called the disciples, He told them that if they followed Him, He would make them fishers of men (Mt. 4:19). People who are like Jesus seek to save the lost (Lk. 19:10).

Thus, in the Gospels, disciples of Jesus were people who made a number of personal decisions that meant they were physically present with Jesus. They listened to Him teach, formally and informally. They watched what He did. They were instructed by Him. They imitated Him. They became more and more like Him. They learned to be like Him in the context of a group.

When I was in college, one of my professors had to leave town during the Christmas holidays and his high school-age son had to stay in town. So the professor asked me to stay in his house to chaperone his son. During that brief time, I spent one-on-one time with the teenager, teaching him some things I knew about the Lord. That experience changed his life. As a result, after he graduated from college, he entered a fulltime ministry discipling people. I was so impressed by what happened to him that for the next several years I thought of discipling as one-on-one teaching. After I graduated from seminary, I had a number of individual disciples. Then one day somebody asked me, "Have you ever noticed that there is no such thing as one-on-one discipling and in the New Testament?" Jesus did not disciple people one-on-one. He discipled them in a group. Even the verse in the epistles most often used as the text for making disciples is not describing a one-on-one process. Second Timothy 2:2 is all in the plural! Timothy learned "among many witnesses" (plural), and he was to commit what he learned to men (plural) who were capable of teaching others (plural). From that point on, I discipled people in small groups.

THE BOOK OF ACTS

THE MEANING

Most take "disciple" in Acts as a synonym for Christian (*ISBE*, vol. 2, p. 851, *TDNT*, vol. 4, p. 457), but the term "disciple" means "learner" and, as has been pointed out, there is a difference between being a believer and being a learner. Moreover, in Acts, the term "disciple" designates those who are connected with a church (*cf.* Acts 8:1, with 9:1, 11:26).

THE METHOD

A. B. Luter points out that the only time the verb "make disciples" is used in the book of Acts it is used in connection with Paul's his first missionary journey, which included baptizing (Acts 16:15, 33; 19:5) and teaching (14:21-22). He concludes, "These aspects of discipleship are involved in the establishment of the church at Jerusalem" (Acts 2:41-42; 5:21, 25, 42), Antioch (Acts 11:26; 15:35), Corinth (Acts 18:11), and Ephesus (Acts 20:20) (A. Boyd Luter, Jr., "Discipleship and the Church," *Bibliotheca Sacra*, 137:547, July 1980, p. 270).

Thus, in Acts, disciples are "learners" in the context of a congregation. Discipling in Acts is not one-on-one; it is in a group—the church. The church became the school where the learner received instructions.

THE EPISTLES

THE CONCEPT

The surprise is that the term "disciple" only appears in the Gospels and in the Book of Acts. Neither the noun nor the verb appears in the epistles, not even once. The concept, however, does. As has been pointed out, the word "disciple" means "learner." There is another Greek word for "learn." In Matthew 11:29, a discipleship passage, Jesus invites those who come to Him (Mt. 11:28) to *learn* from Him. The Greek word Jesus uses for "learn," in Matthew 11:29 is the one Paul uses of believers "learning" doctrine (Rom. 16:17), and "learning Christ" (Eph. 4:20). So the *concept* of being a disciple (a learner) is in the epistles, but a different word for learning is used.

So, while the word "disciple" does not occur in the epistles, the concept of learning does. Samra suggests, "After Jesus ascended to heaven, He was no longer physically present with His disciples, which necessitated a change in the idea of discipleship. This change manifested itself in a change in terminology" (Samra, pp. 222-223).

THE METHOD
In the Gospels, people physically traveled with Jesus to learn from Him. They learned by listening to Him teach and by watching what He did. It was imperative that those who learned from Him be with Him. In other words, they could not learn by lecture alone. They learned by listening and imitating Him. Likewise, in the epistles, believers "learn" both by instruction and imitation. Paul says, "Imitate me, just as I also imitate Christ" (1 Cor. 11:1; see also Gal. 4:12; 2 Thess. 3:7-9; Phil. 3:17; Phil. 4:9; Heb. 13:7; 3 Jn. 11). Even though Paul acknowledged he had shortcomings (Phil. 3:12), he still invited others to follow him (Phil. 3:17). The elders are the examples (1 Pet. 5:1-5), but Jesus is the model. Believers imitate men only as those men imitate Jesus in suffering and service (1 Cor. 11:1).

Jerry Seinfeld, a father of three, says, "Kids are not going to do what you tell them to do or think like you tell them to think. Kids are watching how you deal with the waiter or that handyman, and they are probably more likely to imitate you" (*Parade Magazine*, February 14, 2010, p. 5).

THE RESULT
The result is also the same. In the Gospels, the disciples become just like their teacher, Jesus, who said, "A disciple is not above his teacher, but everyone who is perfectly trained will be like his teacher" (Lk. 6:40). Paul told the Ephesians that gifted men were to equip the saints for their work of ministry (Eph. 4:11-12). The word translated "perfectly trained" in Luke 6:40 is the same as the word rendered "equipped" in Ephesians 4:12. What Jesus spoke of in the Gospels, gifted men do in the epistles. Hence, in the Gospels, the result of discipleship is Christ-likeness and in the epistles the result of training/equipping is Christ-likeness. (also Rom. 8:29; 1 Cor. 15:49; 2 Cor. 3:18; Eph. 4:13-15; Col. 3:9-10; 1 Jn. 3:2).

Samra concluded, "Discipleship is the process of becoming like Christ. During the time of Christ this is accomplished by literally following Him and hearing what He taught and watching what He did. After Jesus' ascension, the process of becoming like Christ involves studying what He said and did and imitating His example. It also involves seeing Christ-likeness lived out in mature believers and becoming more Christ-like through imitating them" (Samra, pp. 225-226).

SUMMARY

In the finest sense of the term, disciples are baptized believers, who are learning to be like Christ in the context of a spiritual community, namely, the church.

There is a personal and congregational side to being a disciple. The spiritual life requires depending on the Lord for eternal life, deciding to get baptized, deeply desiring to be like Him, denying yourself as the authority in life, daily doing God's will, and diligently practicing believing and obeying the Lord. It is not following rules; it is following the Lord. It is not about regulations: it is about a relationship with the Lord.

Disciples are "learners" in the context of a congregation. The church became the school where the learner received instructions. Discipling is not one-on-one; it is in a group—the church. In Hebrews 3:12, believers are warned against having an evil heart of unbelief. Then instead of saying, "Make sure you believe," the author says, "Exhort one another daily" (Heb. 3:13). Believers need a congregation.

CHAPTER EIGHT

THE MEANS OF THE SPIRITUAL LIFE
THE WORD

A s a young believer, I heard conflicting opinions as to what I was to do to live a spiritual life. On the one hand, I was told to get going for the Lord. On the other hand, I was told to let go and let God do it all. Frankly, it was all very confusing to me.

Theologians teach that the spiritual life, called the doctrine of sanctification, is the work of God, Who uses means to bring believers to spiritual maturity. Preachers make it sound as if it is the work of the believer. What is God's part and what is my part? Does it all depend on the Lord or does it all depend on me? Am I to be passive or am I to be active?

Let's review. The goal of the spiritual life is Christ-like maturity. The foundation is the baptism of the Holy Spirit, which is, being united to Christ. The pattern is a process of growth; it is a process of putting off vices and putting on virtues. The requirement is having such a deep desire to be like Christ that believers deny themselves as the authority, daily do the will of God, and diligently follow and obey in the context of a spiritual community.

The next logical question is, "What are the means by which we get to spiritual maturity?" God uses several means. This chapter will focus on His use of the Word. Other means will be described later.

THE PROVISION

STATEMENT
God sanctifies believers. Paul says, "Now may the God of peace Himself sanctify you completely; and may your whole spirit, soul, and body be preserved blameless at the coming of our Lord Jesus Christ" (1 Thess. 5:23). To sanctify believers,

God has provided His Word. Speaking to the Father, Jesus says, "Sanctify them by Your truth. Your word is truth" (Jn. 17:17).

EXPLANATION

Evans says, "How does the Word of God sanctify? By revealing sins; by awakening conscience; by revealing the character of Christ; by showing the example of Christ; by affecting the influences and power of the Holy Spirit; and by setting forth spiritual motives and ideals" (William Evans, *Great Doctrines of the Bible*, p. 169).

THE PROCESS

DESIRE THE WORD

Believers need to respond to the God-given Word. For starters, Peter says, "Therefore, laying aside all malice, all deceit, hypocrisy, envy, and all evil speaking, as newborn babes, desire the pure milk of the word, that you may grow thereby" (1 Pet 2:1-2). Believers are to desire the Word. When we are born spiritually, we are born spiritual babes, who need spiritual milk to grow. The Word of God is the milk that enables spiritual babes to develop spiritually.

There's a story about a proud young man who came to Socrates asking for wisdom. "O great Socrates, I come to you for wisdom." Socrates led the young man through the streets, to the sea, and chest deep into the water. Then he asked, "What do you want?" "Wisdom," said the young man with a smile.

Socrates put hands on the man's shoulders and pushed him under the water. Thirty seconds later Socrates let him up. "What do you want?" he asked again. "Wisdom," the young man sputtered. Socrates pushed him under again. Thirty seconds passed, thirty-five. Forty. Socrates let him up. The man was gasping. "What do you want, young man?" Between heavy, heaving breaths, the fellow wheezed, "Wisdom."

Socrates jammed him under again. Forty seconds passed. Fifty. "What do you want?" "Air!" he screeched. "I need air!" "When you want wisdom as you have just wanted air, then you will have wisdom."

"C. S. Lewis gave us the following insight: Our Lord finds our desires not too strong, but too weak. We are half-hearted creatures, fooling about with drink and sex and ambition when infinite joy is offered to us, like an ignorant child who wants to go on making mud pies in the slum because he cannot imagine what is meant by the offer of a holiday at the sea. We are far too easily pleased" (Michael Horton, Ed., *The Agony of Deceit*. Moody Press, 1990, p. 49).

RECEIVE THE WORD
James says, "Therefore lay aside all filthiness and overflow of wickedness, and receive with meekness the implanted word, which is able to save your souls" (Jas. 1:21). To receive the Word with meekness means to receive it with a teachable spirit.

Some receive the Word, but with an argumentative spirit. When they hear what God says, they want to argue with it. They have three or four reasons for why they can't do that, or why it won't work (maybe the reasons should be called excuses). Some receive the Word with an analytical spirit. When they hear what God says they respond by saying, "That's interesting," and begin to analyze and study it. When they're done, they know what God said, but they have not done what God said. Then there are those blessed saints who receive the Word with an agreeable spirit. The minute they hear the Word they say, "I agree," and do it. James says that is the way to receive the Word, meekly with a teachable spirit.

MEDITATE ON THE WORD
If there is a "method" to the spiritual growth, it is meditation (Jos. 1:8; Ps. 1:2). The Greek word translated "continue" in James 1:25 is not the usual Greek word for "continue." This particular word literally means "to continue beside." Alford refers to Wiesinger's remarks that the idea is not so much of continuing in the sense of observing it in action as it is the sense of observing it in attention. In other words, this is a reference to meditation. After observing carefully what the Word says, a believer needs to linger *beside* it, *thinking through* what it means and how to apply it.

To say the same thing another way, in order to grow, believers need knowledge. That is why Peter says, "Add to your faith virtue, to virtue knowledge" (2 Pet. 1:5). From the Word of God, children of God get knowledge about the will of God. It is that knowledge of God's will that is essential for spiritual growth.

BELIEVE THE WORD
The spiritual life is lived by faith (Rom. 1:17; Heb. 10:38). The writer to the Hebrews says that the Israelites were given promises concerning entering the land, "but the word which they heard did not profit them, not being mixed with faith in those who heard *it*" (Heb. 4:2).

OBEY THE WORD

Another critical means of the spiritual life is obedience. Paul says, "Do you not know that to whom you present yourselves slaves to obey you are that one's slaves whom you obey, whether of sin to death or of obedience to righteousness?" (Rom. 6:16; see also 6:19, 22). Believers can obey or they can disobey the Lord. If they sin, death is the result. If they obey, righteousness is the result. James says the same thing, "But be doers of the word, and not hearers only, deceiving yourselves" (Jas. 1:22). Like Paul, James teaches that if believers obey, righteousness will result (Jas. 1:19).

Obedience requires effort. Believers will never grow by passive surrender alone. There must be an active obedience. Paul says "Exercise yourself toward godliness. For bodily exercise profits a little, but godliness is profitable for all things, having promise of the life that now is and of that which is to come. This *is* a faithful saying and worthy of all acceptance. For to this *end* we both labor and suffer reproach, because we trust in the living God, who is *the* Savior of all men, especially of those who believe" (1 Tim. 4:7b-10).

An eight-year old boy named Dominic DeCarlo went on a skiing trip with his father. Somehow Dominic got lost. More than 90 people conducted an all-night search for a small boy lost on a snowy mountain. As each hour passed, the search party and the boy's family became more and more concerned for his safety and survival. By dawn, they had found no trace of him. Two helicopter crews joined the search and within fifteen minutes had spotted ski tracks. A ground team followed the tracks, which changed to small footprints. The footprints led to a tree where the boy was found—alive. Despite spending the night in freezing temperature, he didn't freeze. Dominic's father had told him what to do if he ever became lost. The son did exactly what his father said. He protected himself from possible frostbite and hypothermia by snuggling up to a tree and covering himself with branches. He never would have thought of doing this on his own; he was simply obeying his wise and loving father.

Spiritual growth takes desire, but desire is not enough. Solomon says, "The soul of a lazy *man* desires, and *has* nothing; but the soul of the diligent shall be made rich" (Prov. 13:4). The lazy soul has desire, but that is all. "He would be wise without study and rich without labor" (Bridges). I would add "spiritual without obedience."

THE PROBLEM

KNOWLEDGE

In order to grow, believers need knowledge, but Paul warns, "Knowledge puffs up" (1 Cor. 8:1). If some kinds of knowledge lead to pride instead of maturity, what kind of knowledge produces spiritual growth? Peter says, "Grow in the grace and knowledge *of our Lord and Savior Jesus Christ*" (2 Pet. 3:18, italics added). Believers need knowledge of how to be like Christ. That comes by contemplating what Christ is like in the Word. Paul says, "But we all, with unveiled face, beholding as in a mirror the glory of the Lord, are being transformed into the same image from glory to glory, just as by the Spirit of the Lord" (2 Cor. 3:18). As believers focus on the Lord in the Word, they are transformed by the Holy Spirit (2 Cor. 3:18; see Rom. 12:2). In short, believers need truth that transforms.

This contemplation of Christ is more than just thinking about Him once in a while. Paul says, "For those who live according to the flesh set their minds on the things of the flesh, but those who live according to the Spirit *the things of the Spirit*" (Rom. 8:5, italics added). The Greek word translated "set their minds" in Romans 8:5 includes the thinking and the will, and even the emotions (Godet; Hodge). Cranfield says it also includes one's outlook, assumptions, values, desires, and purposes (Cranfield, p. 286). The means of the spiritual life is a life of meditation on the Word of God to the point that we have our minds, emotions, will, assumptions, values, and purposes renewed.

OBEDIENCE

Believers need obedience, but there are two kinds of obedience. The obedience the Lord desires is not a legalistic obedience to rules and regulations. It is loving obedience. In the Upper Room Discourse, Jesus says, "If you love Me, keep My commandments" (Jn. 14:15). He also says, "He who has My commandments and keeps them, it is he who loves Me. And he who loves Me will be loved by My Father, and I will love him and manifest Myself to him" (Jn. 14:21) and "If anyone loves Me, he will keep My word; and My Father will love him, and We will come to him and make Our home with him" (Jn. 14:23). The motivation for the spiritual life is love for the Lord. The obedience that resulted in genuine godliness is loving obedience. This is not legal obedience to a set of laws or rules. It is loving obedience to a person.

EFFORT

Believers need to put forth effort, but at the same time, they must depend on the Lord. Jesus says, "Without Me you can do nothing" (Jn. 15:5). It is believing what He says in His Word and depending on Him for the power to do it. Paul says "I have been crucified with Christ; it is no longer I who live, but Christ lives in me; and the *life* which I now live in the flesh I live by faith in the Son of God, who loved me and gave Himself for me" (Gal. 2:20). Walking by faith is trusting the Lord for the strength to do His will.

Spiritual growth takes effort, but effort is not enough. It takes the grace of God. As the songwriter says, "Trust and obey for there is no other way to be happy (spiritual) in Jesus, than to trust and obey." As we trust and obey, God works in our lives.

SUMMARY

God uses His Word to bring believers to spiritual maturity, but believers must cooperate with Him by meditating on, believing, and obeying the Word.

You have to make choices and you have to put forth effort to think about and do what the Word says. At the same time, you must trust the Lord to give you the strength to do what He says. It is a life of faith, believing what God says and lovingly obeying Him by trusting Him for the grace to do His will.

God gives us His Word and His strength. Our part is to saturate our mind with the wisdom of God, believe what God says, and trust Him for the power to do it. Simply put, we believe and obey the Word of God by trusting the God of the Word.

Some see the spiritual life as if it is like rowing a boat; it all depends on them. Others say it is more like a raft; we are passive while God does all the work. The spiritual life is more like operating a sailboat. We do our part of trimming the sails and the wind (the Holy Spirit) does the real work.

It is like growing a garden. We must hoe as if it all depends on us, because it does. We must pray as if it all depends on God, because it does.

CHAPTER NINE

THE MEANS OF THE SPIRITUAL LIFE
THE HOLY SPIRIT

Suppose you worked for a wealthy man, who wanted you to do a job for him a thousand miles from where you lived. One of the things he would have to do is get you from where you are to where you needed to be. He could use one of several means to get you where he wanted you. He could have you walk. He could have you drive. Or he could have you fly.

Likewise, God the Father wants us to move from being spiritual children to being spiritual adults. To get that accomplished, He uses means. Those means include the Word of God and the Spirit of God.

There is a great deal of confusion and even controversy concerning the work of the Holy Spirit. Believers discuss and sometimes debate the baptism of the Holy Spirit and the filling of the Holy Spirit. We have looked at the baptism of the Holy Spirit. Let's look at other works of the Holy Spirit, including the filling of the Holy Spirit.

THE PROVISION

On the night before He was crucified, Jesus told the disciples in the upper room that although He was about to depart, He would not leave them orphans (Jn. 14:18). He promised to send them "another Helper," the Spirit of truth, who would abide with them forever (Jn. 14:16-17). Having given believers new life, and taken up residence in them, as well as sealing them and placing them into the body of Christ, the Holy Spirit is now in a position to "help" believers. More specifically, He teaches, enables, and transforms.

TEACHES

Several passages speak of the teaching ministry of the Holy Spirit. In the upper room, Jesus told the Apostles, "The Helper, the Holy Spirit, whom the Father will send in My name, He will teach you all things, and bring to your remembrance all things that I said to you" (Jn. 14:26; see also Jn. 16:12-15). Jesus spoke this to the disciples and it has its primary fulfillment in them. The Holy Spirit guided *them* into *all* truth. Under His guidance, some of them wrote Scripture (2 Pet. 1:21). Matthew and John wrote about Jesus' words, Peter and Jude wrote some of the "all things." The Holy Spirit teaches believers through the Word He inspired.

Also, God has given the gift of teaching to some believers (Rom. 12:7). The Holy Spirit teaches through teachers. John says, "The anointing which you have received from Him abides in you, and you do not need that anyone teach you; but as the same anointing teaches you concerning all things, and is true, and is not a lie, and just as it has taught you, you will abide in Him" (1 Jn. 2:27). The believers to whom John was writing had been taught (1 Jn. 2:12-14). Therefore they did not need teachers to teach them about the subject about which John was speaking.

In the final analysis, the Holy Spirit teaches believers today through the Word He inspired. He opens the minds of individual believers as they meditate on the Word (Ps. 119:18) and He uses human teachers, who are faithful to the Word the Holy Spirit inspired. The Spirit of truth (Jn. 16:13) guides us into the truth (Jn. 16:13), which is the Word of truth (Jn. 17:17). The Holy Spirit brings to "your remembrance" the Word (Jn. 14:26).

The founder of Dallas Seminary, Dr. Lewis Sperry Chafer, began every school year with a message in chapel in which he said, "There is a faculty of One here, that is, the Holy Spirit."

EMPOWERS

The Holy Spirit empowers (Acts 1:8). Paul speaks of the believer being "strengthened with might through the Spirit in the inner man" (Eph. 3:16). As believers trust the Lord (Eph. 3:17), they comprehend the love of Christ (Eph. 3:18-19), and are filled with all the fullness of God (Eph. 3:19), "according to the power that works in" them (Eph. 3:20).

TRANSFORMS

The Holy Spirit transforms. The Greek word translated "transformed" only appears twice in the New Testament. Paul speaks of being "transformed by the renewing of your mind" (Rom. 12:2) and "But we all, with unveiled face, beholding as in a mirror the glory of the Lord, are being transformed into the same image from glory to glory, just as by the Spirit of the Lord" (2 Cor. 3:18). As believers behold the glory of the Son of God in the Word of God, the Spirit of God gradually transforms them into the image of the Lord. As their minds are renewed by the Holy Spirit, they are transformed into the image of Christ.

In the White Mountains of New Hampshire is a famous pass known as Franconia Notch. Years ago, high on one of the rocky walls protruded a granite formation that resembled the profile of an old man looking over the valley (it collapsed in May 2003). It was called "The Old Man of the Mountain." Nathaniel Hawthorne wrote a story based on that rock formation called "The Legend of the Great Stone Face."

According to the story, a boy named Ernest lived in the valley beneath the great stone face. His mother told him about an ancient legend. She said, "Someday a man will arise, born in this neighborhood whose countenance will resemble the great stone face which you see on the side of that distant mountain." As Ernest looked, he saw in the rock what appeared to be the features of a fine and noble man. From that time in his early years, he spent time concentrating on that inspiring sight. He longed for the day when he could see a real face as kind and as wise as the one that appeared in the rock. Carefully he scrutinized individuals within the village like Mr. Gathergold, General Blood and Thunder and the one called "The "Poet." Each time, however, he was disappointed, yet he never became discouraged in his search, cheerfully performing his daily duties and always seeking to help others. Over the years he gained the respect and admiration of all who knew him. One evening, while he was speaking to a group of his neighbors, the setting sunlit up his countenance. Suddenly, the man called "The Poet" pointed to him and exclaimed, "Look, there's the man who resembles the great stone face." After looking at the image in the mountain and looking for an individual who bore that resemblance, Ernest had become like the Great Stone Face.

The point of the story is that whatever we look on with approval, we become like. Add to that the work of the Holy Spirit and you have how believers are transformed over time into the image of Christ.

THE PROCESS

DEAL WITH SIN

Paul says, "Do not grieve the Holy Spirit of God, by whom you were sealed for the day of redemption" (Eph. 4:30). What grieves the Holy Spirit? In a word—sin. Look at the next verse: "Let all bitterness, wrath, anger, clamor, and evil speaking be put away from you, with all malice" (Eph. 4:31). Notice, it is not just major sins of action that grieve the Holy Spirit. It is what we think of as minor sins of attitude. One of the symbols of the Holy Spirit is a dove. A car would scare doves away, but so will tossing a peanut on the ground in front of them. Likewise, the Holy Spirit is sensitive to what we think of as peanut-sized sins. We need to deal with sins, big and small, by confessing them (1 Jn. 19) and replacing them (Eph. 4:32).

DO THE WILL OF GOD

Paul commands, "Do not quench the Spirit" (1 Thess. 5:19). The word "quench" means "to extinguish, to put out." It was used of putting out a fire. The Spirit, here, refers to the activity of the Spirit or the operation of the gifts of the Spirit. In other words, Paul is saying, "Do not prohibit the free exercise of spiritual gifts in the assembly." We quench the Holy Spirit when we do not do the will of God. So, in essence, this is saying, "Do the will of God."

DEPEND ON THE HOLY SPIRIT

Paul says, "Walk in the Spirit, and you shall not fulfill the lust of the flesh" (Gal. 5:16). How do we walk in the Spirit? Some argue that walking in the Spirit is regulating one's life by the rule/direction of the Holy Spirit. Galatians 5:25 says "let us also walk in the Spirit." The Greek word translated "walk" in verse 25 means to "walk in line." The Holy Spirit gives believers the rule, the direction by which to order their lives. This is done through the Word of God, which the Spirit of God inspired. In Galatians 5, that rule/direction is love.

Another possibility is that walking in the Spirit means "walking by means of" the Holy Spirit; that is, walking with the help of the Holy Spirit. Believers obey the Word of God by being dependent upon the Holy Spirit for enablement. The word "walk," which denotes effort, seems to be the opposite of dependence, but maybe that is the concept Paul means to convey. It is the picture of a man walking on crutches. There is effort and dependence all at the same time.

BE DOMINATED BY THE HOLY SPIRIT

Paul says, "And do not be drunk with wine, in which is dissipation; but be filled with the Spirit" (Eph. 5:18). The filling of the Holy Spirit is mentioned in the Old Testament, in the Gospel of Luke, in Acts, and in Ephesians 5:18. It is only rarely spoken of in the Bible and the only place it is mentioned in the epistles is different than the rest of the references. To further complicate matters, the verse in the epistles is difficult to interpret.

In the Old Testament, the filling of the Spirit was a sovereign act of God for a specific service (Ex. 31:3-5; 35:31-35). Sometimes it was temporary (Num. 11:17, 25-26) and, apparently, sometimes it was more permanent (Num. 27:18; 1 Sam. 16:13). It was also associated with prophesying (Num. 11:25). It was not the normal experience of the daily lives of the Old Treatment saints.

In the Gospel of Luke, the filling seems to be a special work of the Holy Spirit. John the Baptist is said to be filled with the Spirit *from his mother's womb* (Lk. 1:15, italics added). When Elizabeth (Lk. 1:41) and Zacharias (Lk. 1:67) are said to be filled with the Holy Spirit they speak the Word of God (Lk. 1:42-55 and Lk. 1:67-79). Zacharias is said to prophesy (Lk. 1:67). The only other person said to be filled with the Spirit in the Gospel of Luke is Jesus, who is said to be filled with wisdom (Lk. 2:40), as well as the Holy Spirit (Lk. 4:1). These four are the only ones said to be filled with the Spirit in the Gospel of Luke and, therefore in the Gospels. In other words, in the Gospel of Luke, not many experienced the filling; it was a special work only a few experienced.

In the Book of Acts, believers were filled with the Holy Spirit on the day of Pentecost and spoke with other tongues (Acts 2:4). Again, the filling of the Spirit is connected with inspired utterances, in this case, speaking in other languages [Marshall says that the verb translated "addressed" ("said" in Acts 2:14) can be used of inspired utterance; see also Acts 2:17-18; 11:28]. When Peter was filled with the Spirit, He immediately spoke the Word of God (Acts 4:8). The believers who were filled with the Holy Spirit "spoke the Word of God with boldness" (Acts 4:31). The Seven were full of the Holy Spirit and wisdom (Acts 6:3). Stephen was full of faith (Acts 6:5, 6:8), the Holy Spirit (Acts 6:5, 7:55), and wisdom (Acts 6:5). Paul was filled with the Spirit (Acts 9:17) and spoke the Word of God (Acts 13:9). Barnabas was full of the Holy Spirit and faith (Acts 11:24). Disciples are said to be filled "with joy and with the Holy Spirit" (Acts 13:52), that is, they were filled with joy, which comes from the indwelling Holy Spirit (Bruce).

According to Ice, Luke uses the verb "fill" eight times to describe an event of filling (see "filled with the Spirit" in Lk. 1:15, 41, 67; Acts 2:4; 4:8, 31; 9:7; 13:9). Ice explains that in the Greek text, the word "filled" is constructed in such a way to emphasize an event, not a state. It is an instantaneous filling mostly dealing with prophetic utterance. There were no conditions; the recipients were filled by the Spirit as a sovereign work of God (the passive voice of the verb). Evidently, it was repeatable (Peter in Acts 2:4 and in Acts 4:31 and Paul in Acts 9:17 and Acts 13:9). The purpose of the filling was for special prophetic activity or for boldness in their witness of the Word of God. The fillings lasted as long as it took to accomplish the given task (Peter and Paul). Ice concludes that in each of these cases, the filling of the Holy Spirit was a sovereign work of God. There were no conditions and no one is ever commanded to seek it. He adds that since these fillings produced prophetic utterances, which only occurred in the first century, there are no such sovereign fillings today.

According to Ice, Luke uses the adjective "full" five times and the verb as an adjective participial form appears once to describe an abiding condition (Lk. 4:1; Acts 6:3, 5; 7:55; 11:24; 13:52). Ice claims that the difference between the words Luke uses for special filling and the abiding condition is that the special filling indicates that the *action* of filling has *occurred*, while the abiding condition indicates that a *state* of fullness has been *achieved*. In other words, this is like saying a man is "full of wisdom." He does not become full instantaneously to be wise. Rather, he is exceedingly wise and therefore is said to be full of wisdom. Hence, people full of the Holy Spirit are those who consistently exhibits the work of the Holy Spirit in their lives, which indicates that their state did not come instantaneously (as in a sovereign filling), but through a growing process (Tommy Ice, "The Filling of the Holy Spirit: A Quality of Life," *Chafer Theological Seminary Journal Volume*, vol. 2. pp. 6-11).

In the writings of Luke, the filling of the Spirit is associated with speaking an inspired utterance (Lk. 1:41, 1:67; Acts 2:14; see also Acts 11:28), wisdom (Lk. 2:40; Acts 6:3, 5), faith (Acts 6:5, 8; 11:24), and joy (Acts 13:52).

The one reference to the filling of the Spirit in the epistles is in Ephesians 5:18, which simply says, "Be filled with the Spirit." It should be immediately obvious that there is a difference between what Luke calls the filling of the Spirit and what Paul is speaking about here. For example, John the Baptist was filled with the Holy Spirit in his mother's womb. That was a sovereign act of God; John did not do anything. Paul, however, commands believers to be filled; they are somehow involved. Furthermore, the Greek construction in Ephesians 5:18 is different than the one used by Luke.

Pardon the pun, but Paul's command is filled with problems. In the Greek text, the construction of "be filled with the Spirit" is unusual (Eadie). One commentator says "There is a certain strangeness about the construction in Greek" (Foulkes). There is no article before the word "spirit" and the preposition "with" is "in." Thus, the Greek text reads, "Be filled *in* Spirit" (see *Young's Literal Translation*). There are several suggested explanations of this construction.

1. Be filled *with the Spirit*

Despite the fact that the Greek text reads "be filled in Spirit," virtually all English translations render it, "Be filled *with* the Spirit." It is commonly assumed that this imperative means that believers are to be filled *with* the Holy Spirit, as if the Holy Spirit is the substance with which one is filled, like a glass filled with water. This particular Greek construction does not mean "Be filled *with* the Spirit" (Hoehner). If that was what Paul intended, he would have used another Greek construction (Robinson). As F. F. Bruce points out, "Paul does not say, 'Become full of the Spirit,' but 'Be filled in Spirit.'"

2. Be filled *in the sphere of the Spirit*

Others insist that the interpretation is being filled in the realm of the Holy Spirit (Oepke, *TDNT*, 2, 1964, pp. 540-41). The idea of sphere is in Romans 8:9, where Paul says believers are not "in the flesh, but in the Spirit." What does it mean to be filled in the sphere of the Holy Spirit? In Ephesians 5, the filling is associated with walking in wisdom and in understanding the will of God. In fact, before Paul mentions being filled, he says, "Therefore do not be unwise, but understand what the will of the Lord is" (Eph. 5:17). The sphere of the Holy Spirit, the author of the written Word of God, is the will and wisdom of God.

In the Scripture, the Holy Spirit is repeatedly connected to wisdom. Isaiah wrote, "There shall come forth a Rod from the stem of Jesse, and a Branch shall grow out of his roots. The Spirit of the LORD shall rest upon Him, The Spirit of wisdom and understanding, The Spirit of counsel and might, The Spirit of knowledge and of the fear of the LORD (Isa. 11:1-2). Jesus was said to be filled with wisdom (Lk. 2:40) before it is recorded that He was filled with the Holy Spirit (Lk. 4:1). When a problem arose in the church in Jerusalem, the apostles instructed the believers to "seek out from among you seven men of good reputation, full of the Holy Spirit and wisdom, whom we may appoint over this business" (Acts 6:3). They chose Stephen and six others (Acts 6:5). Later the unbelievers to whom Stephen spoke "were not able to resist the wisdom and the Spirit by which he spoke" (Acts 6:10).

Furthermore, in Ephesians 5:18, Paul says "be filled with the Spirit" and says that one of the results is singing. In Colossians 3:16, he says, "Let the word of Christ dwell in you richly," and says one of the result is singing. It has been suggested that since the result of being filled with the Spirit and the

Word dwelling in believers richly both result in the same thing, they are the same thing.

3. Be filled *by means of the Spirit*

The Greek preposition translated "in" means "by means of" in Luke 22:49 (see "Shall we strike with the sword" in Lk. 22:49; Moule, *Idiom Book*, pp. 76-77; Hoehner). Robinson translates it, "Let your fullness be that which comes through the Holy Spirit." Bruce renders it, "Let your fullness be that which the Holy Spirit produces." If that is the meaning, the content of the filling is not specifically stated, but it may refer to the fullness of the moral excellence and the power of God mentioned in Ephesians 1:23 (Hoehner).

Frankly, the Greek construction of this command can mean, "Be filled *in* the Holy Spirit" or "Be filled *by* the Spirit." Robinson says the sequence of thought appears to be, "Find your fullness through a higher instrument or in a higher sphere" adding, "It is difficult to distinguish between the fullness which comes through the Spirit and the fullness which consists in being full of the Spirit."

4. Be filled *in and by means of the Spirit*

Still others combine the concepts of "in" and "by" (Alford; Ellicott; Fee). Alford concludes, let the Spirit "be the region in, and the ingredient with which you are filled." That view has been criticized as being a "needless refinement" (Salmond), but maybe this unusual phrase was chosen to combine the concepts of both "in" and "by." From other passages, this much is clear: the Holy Spirit empowers believers (Eph. 3:16).

The Holy Spirit works in the lives of believers as they pray, In fact, the spiritual life is a life of prayer. Paul says we are to pray without ceasing (1 Thess. 5:17). Several passages speak of "calling on the Lord." Paul says, "Whoever calls on the name of the LORD shall be saved" (Rom. 10:13). The salvation spoken of here is salvation from the power of sin, not the penalty of sin. Peter says, "And if you call on the Father, who without partiality judges according to each one's work, conduct yourselves throughout the time of your stay *here* in fear" (1 Pet. 1:17). Paul told Timothy, "Flee also youthful lusts; but pursue righteousness, faith, love, peace with those who call on the Lord out of a pure heart" (2 Tim. 2:22). As we call on the Lord, He grants us the grace to do what He says. "Let us therefore come boldly to the throne of grace, that we may obtain mercy and find grace to help in time of need" (Heb. 4:16). The Holy Spirit was sent to help. As we call, He helps.

THE PROBLEM

CRISIS

There has been a great deal of confusion concerning the filling of the Holy Spirit. One of the misconceptions is that the filling of the Spirit is something that happens "once for all" or in a crisis experience that may be repeated. The filling of the Spirit is not a "once-for-all experience" (Foulkes) or a crisis experience. The command in Ephesians 5:18 is in the present tense!

CONTROL

Another misunderstanding concerns the concept of control. Many say that the filling of the Holy Spirit means the control of the Holy Spirit. For example, Hodge says, "Men are said to be filled with wine when completely under its influence; so they are said to be filled with the Spirit when he controls all their thoughts, feelings, words, and actions." There is truth to that concept, but it needs to be clarified.

It is sometimes said that when believers are filled with the Spirit, they are no longer in control, but they are under the control of the Holy Spirit. Believers are to get off the throne of their lives and put Jesus on the throne. Or, to use another illustration, the filling is like driving a car. When you are in the driver's seat, you are in control; what you must do is get in the back seat and let Jesus drive the car. The point of both of these illustrations is that in this view of the filling of the Spirit, Jesus is in *total control* and you are passive, and not in control at all.

The problem with that explanation of the control of the Spirit is that it teaches that believers are not in control of themselves, which is contrary to the Scripture. The fruit of the Spirit is *self*-control. Besides, it doesn't work.

Years ago, I was speaking for a pastor who had recently discovered the "wonderful truth of the filling of the Spirit." He was sharing his experience with me as we were riding down the highway in his car. He was driving; I was sitting beside him in the front seat. In the midst of the conversation, I said to him, "Are you filled with the Spirit right this minute?" He said, "I have met all the conditions for the filling of the Spirit." I said, "You're fudging. I want to know, are you filled with the Spirit right this minute?" He said, "I think I have every reason to believe that the Spirit of God has filled me." I said, "You're hedging. Are you filled with the Spirit?" He finally had to admit that he must be filled with the Spirit, because he had met the conditions he was taught for the filling. I said, "Now let me clarify. That means that the Lord is in control of you right now and you are not in control of yourself." He said, "Yes, that's right." I said, "I have two problems with that. The first is that if that is true, what is coming out of your mouth are the words of God, which means what you say is tantamount to inspiration. The second problem I have with that is, why are you speeding?"

It would be better to say that Holy Spirit is in control in the sense that, He ultimately determines what is done. A better illustration of the "control" of the Holy Spirit is that you are in the front seat, behind the steering wheel, driving the car, in control; and the Lord is sitting beside you telling you to turn left, to go straight, to turn right. In that sense, He is in control, and so are you. That is the filling, or if you will, the control, of the Holy Spirit. The directions He gives us come from the Word of God. It is the Spirit of God, through His Word, that is directing and controlling. Any explanation that suggests a believer is no longer in control is not biblical.

It is often suggested that as a drunken man is out of control, so the believer who is filled with the Spirit is out of control. A drunken man is not totally out of control; he is "under the influence."

SUMMARY

God uses the Holy Spirit to teach, empower, and transform believers into Christ-like maturity, but believers must cooperate with the Holy Spirit by dealing with sin, doing the will of God, and depending on the Holy Spirit of God.

What are the results of the filling of the Spirit? In his one volume commentary on the New Testament, MacDonald writes, "Does a person know when he is filled with Spirit? Actually, the closer we are to the Lord, the more we are conscious of our own complete unworthiness and sinfulness (Isa. 6:1-5). In His presence, we find nothing in our souls to be proud of (Luke 5:8). We are not aware of any spiritual superiority over others, any sense of 'having arrived.' The believer who is filled with the Spirit is occupied with Christ and not with self. At the same time, he may have a realization that God is working in and through his life."

Chafer says being filled with the Spirit is "*conformity* to His mind and will." He goes on to say, "The Spirit's work is to produce Christian character (Gal. 5:22, 23), Christian service by the exercise of a gift (1 Cor. 12:4-7), knowledge of the Scripture through the teaching ministry of the Spirit (John 16:12-15; Rom. 8:14, 16, 26, 27; 1 John 2:27); but in this context (Eph. 5) it has pleased the Spirit to mention only the fact that the Spirit-filled life is one of ceaseless *praise* and *gratitude* (verses 19, 20)" (from Chafer's commentary on Ephesians).

Following the imperative of verse 18 are five participles, usually taken to be the result of being filled in the realm of the Holy Spirit. Pointing to those verses that follow Ephesians 5:18, Wiersbe says that believers who are filled with the Spirit are joyful (Eph. 5:19), thankful (Eph. 5:20), and submissive (Eph. 5:21-33).

The Word of God tells us what to do and the Spirit of God gives us the power to do it. The two work together. As Paul says in 2 Corinthians, "But we all, with unveiled face, beholding as in a mirror the glory of the Lord, are being transformed into the same image from glory to glory, just as by the Spirit of the Lord" (2 Cor. 3:18). The mirror is the Word. As believers focus on the Lord in the Word, the Holy Spirit uses the Word to transform them.

Paul commands believers to be "filled with the Spirit" and says that one of the results is singing (Eph. 5:18-21). In Colossians 3:16, He says, "Let the word of Christ dwell in you richly," and says one of the results is singing. It has been suggested that since the result of being filled with the Spirit and the Word dwelling in believers richly both result in the same thing, they are the same thing. That maybe an oversimplification, but it certainly indicates that both the Word and the Holy Spirit are involved together in the spiritual life.

The biblical approach to being filled with the Holy Spirit is to be filled with the Word until you think like God thinks and you trust Him to give you the grace and strength to do it. Again: *The Word tells us what to do; the Holy Spirit gives us the power to do it.*

It is like your wealthy boss giving you a map and a car to travel a thousand miles. The map tells you where to go and the route to take. The car gets you there, but you must cooperate. You must drive. You decide which road. You can take the road marked out on the map. Or you can go where you want to go. If you take the road the boss told you to take, you do not think about the motor all the time, but the motor provides the power for the trip. This would be an even better illustration if when you take a wrong turn, the car breaks down!

CHAPTER TEN

THE MEANS OF THE SPIRITUAL LIFE

THE PEOPLE

God uses means to bring believers to spiritual maturity. He provides us with His Word and He supplies us with the Holy Spirit. Is that all we need? Could you, on your own, simply master the content of the Word depending on the Lord for His grace, and grow to spiritual maturity? You could learn a lot, but from a New Testament point of view, you could not reach spiritual maturity. What else is needed?

THE PROVISION

EPHESIANS

Paul says, "From whom the whole body, joined and knit together by what every joint supplies, according to the effective working by which every part does its share, causes growth of the body for the edifying of itself in love" (Eph. 4:16). Paul is using the figure of the human body to illustrate the body of Christ. Every part of the body is connected to the head—Christ. As each part fulfills its proper function, the body grows in love. Each individual part contributes to this growth. The growth here is the growth of the whole body, but the growth of the whole body necessitates the growth of all the individuals in it. The point is believers are united to each other and grow together.

COLOSSIANS

Paul says, "For I want you to know what a great conflict I have for you and those in Laodicea, and *for* as many as have not seen my face in the flesh that their hearts may be encouraged, being knit together in love, and *attaining* to all riches of the full assurance of understanding, to the knowledge of the mystery of God, both of the Father and of Christ in whom are hidden all the treasures of wisdom and knowledge" (Col. 2:1-3). Being knit together in love brings full understanding. The expression "knit together" suggests that God's revelation cannot be understood "in isolation from the fellowship of other Christians" (Vaughan). The revelation of God cannot be known apart from the "brotherly love within the community" (Bruce).

HEBREWS

The writer to the Hebrews says, "let us consider one another in order to stir up love and good works, not forsaking the assembling of ourselves together, as *is* the manner of some, but exhorting *one another*, and so much the more as you see the Day approaching" (Heb. 10:24-25).

All of these passages and others teach that God uses people in the spiritual growth of His children. As John Calvin put it, "No member of the body of Christ is endowed with such perfections as to be able, without the assistance of others, to supply his own necessities."

The very nature of being a believer is being united to Jesus Christ and His body, which is the church. Ortberg writes, "A friend of mine was ordering breakfast during a recent trip to the South. He saw grits on the menu, and being a Dutchman who spent most of his life in Michigan, he had never been very clear on the nature of this item. So he asked the waitress, 'What exactly is grit?' Her response was a classic. 'Honey,' she said (in the South, waitresses are required by law to address all customers as 'honey'), 'Honey, they don't come by themselves." Ortberg adds, "Grits don't exist in isolation. No grit is an island, entire unto itself. Every grit is a part of the mainland, a piece of the whole. You can't order a single grit. They're a package deal. 'Call it a clan, call it a tribe, call it a network, call it a family,' says Jane Howard. 'Whatever you call it, whoever you are, you need one.' It is not good for man to be alone. Dallas Willard says, 'The natural condition of life for human beings is reciprocal rootedness in others' Honey, you don't come by yourself" (John Ortberg, *Everybody's Normal Till You Get to Know Them*, pp. 18-19).

THE PROCESS

EDUCATION

God uses believers to educate us. In Ephesians 4, Paul says that God has given gifted believers to the church. "And He Himself gave some to be apostles, some prophets, some evangelists, and some pastors and teachers" (Eph. 4:11). The apostles and prophets were the foundation (Eph. 2:20). In this passage, evangelists minister to saints, not just sinners. In the Greek text, pastor and teacher are inseparably linked together, indicating that these are two characteristics of the same person. Both are governed by one article; the word "the" occurs before "pastors," but not before "teachers." This is indicated in the English translation by the fact that the word "some" is not repeated before the word "teachers." Furthermore, the word "and" between "pastors" and "teachers" is different than the other "ands" in this verse. The word "pastor" literally means "shepherd." Shepherds exercise oversight over the flock; they provide for and protect it; they guide it and guard it. A teacher, of course, is one who gives instruction. In this case, the teacher instructs others in the Word of God (2 Tim. 3:16). These two functions are united in one man. The pastor/teacher leads by feeding and he feeds by teaching the Word of God.

Having mentioned four speaking gifts (1 Pet. 4:11), Paul now turns his attention to the purpose of the gifts. He first gives the immediate purpose, which is "for the equipping of the saints" (Eph. 4:12a). The Greek word translated "equip" means "to mend or repair, to furnish completely, complete, equip, prepare." The meaning here is that of furnishing, completing, preparing, equipping as a ship for a journey. Training is the idea (Lk. 6:40).

Gifted men are to equip saints by ministering the Word to them. Paul told Timothy that all Scripture was inspired and profitable to "thoroughly equip" (1 Tim. 3:16, 17). Therefore, he should minister it to people (2 Tim. 4:1-2).

Calvin said people "are insane, who neglecting this means hope to be perfect in Christ, as is the case with fanatics, who pretend to secret revelations of the Spirit; and the proud, who content themselves with the private reading of the Scriptures, and imagine that they have no need the ministry of the church" (Calvin, cited by Hodge, p. 230). Charles Hodge adds, "If Christ has appointed this ministry of the edification of the body, it is vain to expect that end to be accomplished in any other way" (Hodge, p. 230).

EXAMPLES
God uses examples for us to emulate (1 Cor. 11:1; 1 Pet. 5:3). Children learn by imitation. No one believer is an example of everything. Find the one thing each believer illustrates. The child learns more by eye than the ear.

ENCOURAGEMENT
God uses believers to encourage one another (Heb. 10:24-25). The writer to the Hebrews mentions three things necessary for encouragement.

1. People encourage one another by being there
Hebrews 10:25 says do not forsake the assembly. Later in the Hebrews passage, the author says believers are to exhort one another. The root meaning of the Greek word translated "exhort" means "called alongside."

2. People encourage one another by considering one another
Hebrews 10:24 says "consider one another." The Greek word translated "consider" means "to take note of, perceive, consider carefully." This cannot be done without listening to what the person is saying. The reason for carefully considering the person (Heb. 10:24) is to understand what the person is experiencing. So, before specifically addressing a problem, you must understand it. Ministry is more likely to be effective if the person feels that the one ministering to them understands them. This can be done by identifying with them.

Recently a man sent me an email in which he said Romans 7 was one of his favorite passages of Scripture. He wrote, "Paul opens up about his own struggles with sin and how even though he knows what to do and wants to do it... he constantly does the opposite. Wow, that is powerful stuff. To hear Paul, one of my all-time Bible heroes and no doubt one of the Godliest men in history, say that he struggles with the same things I do... well it's actually kind of encouraging in a weird way."

3. People encourage one another by exhorting one another
Hebrew 10:25 speaks of "exhorting one another." The Greek word rendered "exhort" means, "helper" (see Jn. 14:16, 20; 1 Jn. 2:1).

Other ministries could be discussed. God uses believers to correction and rebuke (2 Tim. 4:2; Titus 1:9) and, if need be, restore (Gal. 6:1).

ENGAGEMENT
You need to be ministered to and you need to minister to others. Paul says gifted believers equip saints "for the work of ministry, for the edifying of the body of Christ" (Eph. 4:12b). God has given commands concerning relating to one another. I once did a series of messages on the "one another" phrase in the epistles. God has given you a gift for you to minister to others.

If you are a believer, you are in the ministry. You have a gift, you are being fed, and you should be working. What ability has God given you? Do have the ability to be nice to someone? Do you have the ability to comfort others in sorrow, or to cheer people who are sick? Has God given you a nugget of wisdom that someone else needs? Do you know how to give counsel to someone? There is a smorgasbord of need and opportunity. There is something you can do. You don't need to wait for a special invitation.

James 1 begins talking about trials, saying that if you respond properly, they will develop maturity in you. That chapter ends talking about you ministering to others. Ministry to others ministers to you. Ministering to others is part of Christ-like maturity.

A student came to a professor complaining that he was not making any progress in his studies. He asked if he should obtain a tutor. He put it in college terms asking if he needed a coach. The wise professor replied, "You do not need a coach; you need a pupil. There is no better way to learn than teaching others."

THE PROBLEM

In discussing the other means of the spiritual life, it has been pointed out that there is a problem. For example, God provides us with His Word. The problem is that believers learn, but do not grow. God provides the Holy Spirit. The problem is that believers want Him to do it all. God has also provides us with a family of believers, but there are problems with that.

NO ATTENDANCE
You cannot be encouraged by others or encourage others unless you are in the assembly of a local church. Do not forsake the assembly.

NO INVOLVEMENT
The problem is that we want to be ministered to, not minister. You can do something, so do it. You can park cars, bake pies, visit the sick, make phone calls or just listen to someone who is hurting. A good listener is harder to find than a good speaker.

WRONG INVOLVEMENT
Fellowship with the wrong group will stunt your growth and fellowship with the right group will fascinate your spiritual growth. It is like the growth of sharks. I have heard that if a small shark is confined to a public aquarium, it will stay a size proportional to the aquarium. Sharks can be physically mature, but only six inches long. If, however, they are turned loose in the ocean, they grow to their normal length of eight feet. Whether that story is true or not, I do not know, but this I do know. Put a new believer in a group of spiritually small Christians and the chances are that the new believer will not grow very

much. On the other hand, put a new believer with mature Christians and the chances are much greater that the new believer will grow. Some Christians are six inches long swimming in small puddles. Others are eight feet long swimming in an ocean.

SUMMARY

God uses the people of God to bring the children of God to spiritual maturity, but believers must minister to one another.

This is a difficult process. People have a way of hurting one another rather than helping one another. One author has described the situation with an analogy:

"The North American Common Porcupine is a member of the rodent family that has around 30,000 quills attached to his body. Each quill can be driven into an enemy, and the enemy's body heat will cause the microscopic barb to expand and become more firmly embedded. The wounds can fester; the more dangerous ones, affecting vital organs, can be fatal.

"The porcupine is not generally regarded as a lovable animal. The Latin name *(erethizon dorsatum)* means "the irritable back," and they all have one. Books and movies celebrate almost every conceivable animal—not just dogs and cats and horses, but also pigs *(Babe;* Arnold Ziffel from the old TV show *Green Acres),* spiders *(Charlotte's Web),* dolphins *(Flipper),* bears *(Gentle Ben),* and killer whales *(Free Willy).* Even skunks have Pepe Le Pew. I don't know of any famous porcupines. I don't know any child who has one for a pet.

"As a general rule, porcupines have two methods for handling relationships: withdrawal and attack. They either head for a tree or stick out their quills. They are generally solitary animals. Wolves run in packs; sheep huddle in flocks; we speak of herds of elephants and gaggles of geese and even a murder of crows. But there is no special name for a group of porcupines. They travel alone.

"Porcupines don't always want to be alone. In the late autumn, a young porcupine's thoughts turn to love. But love turns out to be a risky business when you're a porcupine. Females are open to dinner and a movie only once a year; the window of opportunity closes quickly. And a girl porcupine's "no" is the most widely respected turndown in all the animal kingdom. Fear and anger make them dangerous little creatures to be around.

"This is the Porcupine's Dilemma: How do you get close without getting hurt? This is our dilemma, too. Every one of us carries our own little arsenal.

Our barbs have names like rejection, condemnation, resentment, arrogance, selfishness, envy, contempt. Some people hide them better than others, but get close enough and you will find out they're there. They burrow under the skin of our enemies; they can wound and fester and even kill. We, too, learn to survive through a combination of withdrawal and attack. We, too, find ourselves hurting (and being hurt by) those we long to be closest to.

"Yet we, too, want to get close. We meet neighbors, go on dates, join churches, form friendships, get married, have children. We try to figure out how to get close without getting hurt. We wonder if there isn't a softer, less-barbed creature out there—a mink or an otter, perhaps.

"And of course, we can usually think of a number of particularly prickly porcupines in our lives. But the problem is not just them. I'm somebody's porcupine. So are you" (John Ortberg, *Everybody's Normal Till You Get to Know Them*, pp. 21-22).

"Miracle of miracles: relationship happens—even for porcupines. On rare occasions, one porcupine will share space with another, and they become friends. Once in a great while, one gets raised in captivity and will eat directly from a human hand. Porcupines learn to keep their barbs to themselves. Not only that, they figure out how to get together at least long enough to make sure that another generation will come along. In an image too wonderful to be made up, naturalist David Costello writes, 'Males and females may remain together for some days before mating. They may touch paws and even walk on their hind feet in the so-called 'dance of the porcupines.' Only God could have thought up two porcupines fox-trotting paw-to-paw, where no one but they and he will ever see. It turns out there really is an answer to the ancient question, how do porcupines make love? They pull in their quills and learn to dance" (John Ortberg, *Everybody's Normal Till You Get to Know Them*, pp. 24-25).

This is difficult, but instead of withdrawing; let's dance.

CHAPTER ELEVEN

THE CHALLENGE OF THE SPIRITUAL LIFE

There is a common adage that says, "Two things are certain: death and taxes." That's not exactly correct. It would be more accurate to say that there are three things that are certain: death, taxes, and trouble. Problems are part and parcel of life. The dream of a carefree life is just that. It is a dream. Why is life filled with trouble? How are we supposed to handle trouble, trials, and tribulations? Three passages in the New Testament directly address trials and tribulations: one by James, one by Peter, and one by Paul.

JAMES

James writes, "My brethren, count it all joy when you fall into various trials, knowing that the testing of your faith produces patience. But let patience have *its* perfect work, that you may be perfect and complete, lacking nothing" (Jas. 1:2-4).

TRIALS
James speaks of various trials (1:2). He says "when," not "if." Trials will come. The Greek word translated "various" means "many-colored." Trials come in various colors and shades. Some are a light gray, like an irritation or a disappointment. Others are a dark black, like a divorce or a death. This passage, then, applies to all kinds of trials, from little annoyances which are part of everyday experience to severe suffering. The book of James refers to financial pressure (Jas. 1:9, 27), oppression (Jas. 2:6), disputes (Jas. 4:1), injustice (Jas. 5:1-6), illness (Jas. 5:14), and death (Jas. 1:27).

REJOICE

When trials arrive, the believer is to "count it all joy." The Greek word "count" means "consider" and occurs here in the Greek text is in the aorist tense, implying decisiveness. "All" does not mean "nothing but joy" as if there is no other emotion. It emphasizes the quality of the joy. This joy is a "calm delight," a "cheerfulness" (Strong). James is saying, "Make up your mind to consider this trial as something about which you will be glad."

FAITH

The Greek word for "testing of your faith" only occurs twice in the New Testament: here and in 1 Peter 1:7, where it is translated "the genuineness of your faith." It means "tested, approved." James is talking about tested, approved faith, that is, genuine faith. When trials come, believers are to trust the Lord for grace (2 Cor. 12:7-10).

ENDURE

This approved, genuine faith produces patience. There are two Greek words translated "patience" in the New Testament. One means "patience" proper, while the other means "endurance." The one used in James 1:3 means "endurance." Thus, James 1:3 is saying, "Genuine faith produces endurance."

MATURITY

The Greek word translated "perfect" means "reaching its end, finished, complete, mature." Endurance will make you mature (fully developed), and complete (with all your parts). God wants all of His children complete (having all of their parts) and mature (having all of those parts fully developed). To accomplish that end, He allows trials to come into their lives to either add something to them or develop something that is already in them.

REWARD

Later in the passage, James says, "Blessed is the man who endures temptation; for when he has been approved, he will receive the crown of life which the Lord has promised to those who love Him" (Jas. 1:12). The Greek word translated "temptation" means "temptation, trials." In this verse, it is referring to trials; trials are endured, not temptation. In the next verse, it means "temptation." If believers endure trials, they will receive a reward at the Judgment Seat of Christ.

James is saying, "When trials come, if you trust the Lord, you will endure, grow toward maturity now, and be rewarded later." In other words, trials are for your training and trials are for a trophy.

When a mother eagle builds her nest, she starts with thorns, broken branches, sharp rocks, and a number of other items that seem unsuitable for the project. Then, she lines the nest with a thick padding of wool, feathers, and fur from animals she has killed, making it soft and comfortable for the eggs. By the time the growing birds reach flying age, the comfort of the nest and the luxury of free meals make them quite reluctant to leave. That is when the mother eagle begins "stirring up the nest." She begins pulling up the thick carpet of fur and feathers, bringing the sharp rocks and branches to the surface. As more of the bedding gets plucked up, the nest becomes more uncomfortable for the young eagles. Eventually, this and other urgings prompt the growing eagles to leave their once-comfortable abode and move on to more mature behavior (*Today in the Word*, June 11, 1989). The trial of the nest moves young eagles to move on to maturity.

1 PETER

Peter says, "In this you greatly rejoice, though now for a little while, if need be, you have been grieved by various trials that the genuineness of your faith, *being* much more precious than gold that perishes, though it is tested by fire, may be found to praise, honor, and glory at the revelation of Jesus Christ" (1 Pet. 1:6-7).

TRIALS

Like James, Peter writes about "various trials." He uses the same Greek word for various, which means "many-colored." We speak of "blue Monday" and "black Tuesday." Peter also says that these believers had been *grieved* by these trials. The Greek word rendered "grieved" means "distress, pain." Trials are painful, often because they involve a loss. In fact, the word translated "grieved" here is used in 1 Thessalonians 4:13 of the sorrow of saints at the death of a loved one.

The occasion of 1 Peter was the news of growing opposition and persecution of believers in Asia Minor (1 Pet. 1:6; 3:13-17; 4:12-19; 5:9-10). Hostility and superstition were mounting. These believers were being slandered and attacked because of their faith (1 Pet. 3:14-15). They were being hated because of their withdrawal from sinful practices. Apparently, there were also charges against them of disloyalty to the state (1 Pet. 2:13-17).

GREATLY REJOICE

The startling point Peter makes is that when believers are grieved by all kinds of trials, they are to "greatly rejoice!" They are to be glad when they are sad (Adams). The Greek word rendered "greatly rejoice" denotes intense joy, "to exult, to be overjoyed." Peter uses this word three times in this epistle (1 Pet. 1:6, 8; 4:13). Paul does not use it at all, but it does appear in the Lord's statement, "Rejoice and be exceedingly glad, for great is your reward in heaven" (Mt. 5:12).

FAITH

Our faith is more valuable than gold, but like gold, it is tested. Trials test our faith. The purpose of putting gold through fire is not to see whether or not it is genuine. It is to purify and refine it; the fire burns out the dross. The purpose of the test is to bring out the true nature of the object tested. God tests, that is, tries saints to bring out and develop their faith. Satan tests, that is, tempts, to bring out and develop our flesh. The purpose of these grievous trials is to develop our faith.

The impurity in our faith that the fire of trials burns out is confidence in ourselves (2 Cor. 1:8-9). Trials bring us to the end of ourselves. Trials force us to depend on the Lord. No matter who you are, no matter how intelligent, no matter how talented, no matter how much money you have, no matter how many contacts you have, there will always be a problem that you cannot solve. God will see to it that you are never in a place where you cannot do without Him.

(ENDURANCE)

The word endurance here is in parentheses because, at this point in the process, it is mentioned by James, but it is not mentioned by Peter. Given all that is said in the New Testament on this subject, it is safe to say Peter assumes it (see Paul's discussions of trials, which come next).

GROWTH

Later in this passage, Peter speaks about "receiving the end of your faith—the salvation of your souls" (1 Pet. 1:9). The Greek word translated "salvation" means "deliverance." It is used in the New Testament of our past deliverance from the penalty of sin (see "have been saved" in Eph. 2:8), our present deliverance from the power of sin (see "being saved" in 1 Cor. 1:18), and our future deliverance from the presence of sin (see Christ will appear *for* our salvation in Heb. 9:28). The salvation spoken of in 1 Peter 1:9 is the present deliverance from the power of sin. The Greek word translated "receiving" is in the present tense and means "to receive back," and the Greek word translated "souls" means "life." In other words, as we learn to trust the Lord more and more, we are delivered more and more from the power of sin; our *life* is being saved (for other passages on the salvation of the soul, that is life, see Mt. 16:24-27; Jn. 12:25; Jas, 1:21). In short, we are growing spiritually.

Hence, as believers trust the Lord and rejoice in Him even in the midst of trials, God is paying them back. They are earning the salvation of their life by their faith and rejoicing. The revelation of that salvation awaits the coming of Christ (Pet. 1:5, 7). When believers seek to preserve their life for themselves, they lose, ruin or waste it, but if they lose their life for Christ, they actually save it.

REWARD

The faith that is developed will be rewarded. The reward will be praise, honor, and glory at the Judgment Seat of Christ. Praise is the verbal recognition and approval that will be given. It will be the "well done, good and faithful servant" from the Lord Himself (Mt. 25:21; 1 Cor. 4:5). Honor is the position of distinction, the rank, which will be bestowed (Jn. 12:26). "Glory" means "opinion, reputation, brightness, splendor." Hence, glory is the reputation or splendor that will be enjoyed.

Pain properly handled now produces praise later. Suffering now results in glory later. When in the midst of a trial it is hard to rejoice when we look around at the situation, but we can rejoice when we look ahead (Wiersbe).

A sign on a sundial said, "Without the shadow I am nothing!"

Peter is saying, "When trials come, if you trust the Lord, you will save your life from being wasted now and you will be rewarded later." Trials are for your training and trials are for a trophy.

Through a wall of glass, customers watch Krispy Kreme doughnuts being made. In the words of another, "First the little balls of dough are shot through with a piercing blast of air to create a hole. Then the flat doughnuts are forced to spend time in the "proof box" where they ride a vertical elevator up and down in an atmosphere of heat and humidity. This is what allows the flat dough to rise. Then the soon-to-be delicacies are dropped into hot oil to be cooked thoroughly. As the circular survivors of such an intense ordeal make their way toward the end of the line, they pass through a cascading waterfall of icing. Just as the poor doughnut's trial produces a product of great delight to the customer, the trials God allows in our lives bring about in us what delights him." He is so delighted that He rewards us.

ROMANS

Paul says that we "rejoice in hope of the glory of God. And not only *that*, but we also glory in tribulations, knowing that tribulation produces perseverance; and perseverance, character; and character, hope" (Rom. 5:2b-4).

TRIBULATION

The Greek word translated "tribulations" means "pressure" and is used figuratively of distress, affliction, physical hardship, and sufferings. Today we would use the word "stress." Life is filled with problems. As someone has said, "Life is filled with trouble and then, we die." Those difficulties often provoke complaints, griping, and even murmuring against God.

REJOICE

The Greek word translated "glory" in verse 3 is the same Greek word translated "rejoice" in verse 2. Believers can rejoice, glory, boast, in their present troubles and be jubilant in their future hope.

(FAITH)

The word faith here is in parentheses because at this point in the process, it is mentioned by James and Peter, but is not mentioned by Paul. Given that Paul discussed the faith of Abraham in Romans 4, and what he says next, it is safe to say that Paul assumes faith is part of the process.

ENDURANCE

Paul says that "tribulation produces perseverance." The Greek word translated "perseverance" in Romans 5 is the same Greek word that is translated "endurance" in James 1. Technically, it is not correct that tribulation produces perseverance or endurance. As James points out, and Paul leaves out, when trials and tribulations come, it is faith that produces endurance. Tribulation produces endurance when, in the words of Cranfield, "it is met by faith in God which receives it as God's fatherly discipline" (2 Cor. 4:16, 18; esp. Jas. 1:2-3, which says that the approved part of faith produces endurance). At any rate, Paul teaches that tribulation produces endurance.

CHARACTER

Endurance produces character. The Greek word translated "character" means "approvedness." As believers endure tribulation, they develop qualities and virtues approved by God. Endurance develops "approved character." To add "proven" to character is like adding "sterling" to the word "silver."

REWARD

Character produces hope, a Greek word that means "expectation." Believers "rejoice in hope of the glory of God" (Rom. 5:2). Believers can now boast in the sure expectation of the glory of God. The phrase "the glory of God" can mean either the glory God possesses or the glory He gives to others. According to what Peter says, this is the glory given to believers at the coming of Christ.

Paul is saying, "When tribulations come, if you endure, you will end up with character now and be rewarded later." Trials are for your training and for a trophy.

At the National Prayer Breakfast in Washington, D.C., on February 6, 2003, Dr. Condoleezza Rice, National Security Advisor, said, "American slaves used to sing, 'Nobody knows the trouble I've seen—Glory, Hallelujah!' Growing up, I would often wonder at the seeming contradiction contained in this line. But as I grew older, I came to learn that there is no contradiction at all." She is right; tribulation and glory go together because tribulation enables us to win the glory.

SUMMARY

Believers can rejoice in trials because they know that if they trust God and endure they will grow now and receive glory later. Trials are for your training and trials are for a trophy.

James, Peter, and Paul are saying the same thing. Peter leaves out endurance and Paul leaves out mentioning faith, but all three are saying that when trials come, if we trust the Lord, we will grow toward maturity now and we will be rewarded later. Trials are for your training and for a trophy.

JAMES	TRIALS	REJOICE	FAITH	ENDURE	MATURITY	CROWN OF LIFE
I PETER	TRIALS	REJOICE	FAITH	(ENDURE)	GROWTH	GLORY
ROMANS	TRIBULATIONS	GLORY	(FAITH)	ENDURE	CHARACTER	HOPE OF GLORY

All three put this concept at the beginning of their discussion of the spiritual life. James and Peter obviously put it first. It might not appear that Paul puts it first, but he does. The first four chapters of Romans deal with justification. When he begins to discuss the spiritual life, the first thing he deals with is trials.

The movie *Pearl Harbor*, which blends history and fiction, is about the Japanese attack on Pearl Harbor on December 7, 1941. Following the attack on Pearl Harbor, President Roosevelt (played by Jon Voight), seated in his wheelchair, gathers his cabinet in the War Room of the White House. He is desperate for answers on how the U.S. can strike back. He speaks to the gathered advisors: "We're on the ropes, gentlemen. That's why we have to strike back now. I'm talking about hitting the heart of Japan the way they have hit us."

The head of the Army counters, "Mr. President, Pearl Harbor caught us unawares. We didn't face the facts. This isn't a time for ignoring them again. The Army Air Corps has long-range bombers but no place to launch them. Midway is too far, and Russia won't allow us to launch a raid from there."

The president asks the head of the Navy for his opinion. The admiral is cautious, and again the president is disappointed. Frustrated that his key advisors are unwilling to take risks, President Roosevelt looks over their faces and says: "Gentlemen, most of you did not know me when I had the use of my legs. I was young and proud and arrogant. Now I wonder every hour of my life why God put me in this chair. But when I see defeat in the eyes of my countrymen—in your eyes right now—I start to think that maybe he brought me down for times like these when we all need to be reminded who we are, that we will not give up or give in." A decorated general speaks up: "Mr. President, with all due respect, what you're asking can't be done."

Roosevelt stares back in defiance and without saying a word struggles to pull himself with his braced legs out of his wheelchair. He pushes aside the aide who attempts to help him. At last, exhausted, he stands. He looks at his advisors and declares, "Do not tell me it can't be done!"

God has given you a wheelchair. If you have trust Him and endure, you will have the character it takes to win the victory.

CHAPTER TWELVE

THE ENEMIES: THE WORLD, THE FLESH, AND THE DEVIL

As you have discovered by now, life contains enemies. Subtly and silently termites eat away at your house. Viruses and bacteria invade your body. Likewise, there are enemies to your spiritual life. Like termites and germs, they can damage and destroy your life of fellowship with the Lord.

What are the enemies of our spiritual life? Equally important, what is our defense against these enemies? We use pesticides for termites and antibiotics for bacteria. What do we use for the enemies of our spiritual life?

James speaks of a wisdom that "is earthly, sensual, demonic" (Jas. 3:15). Earthly is that which is of the world. Sensual is of the flesh and demonic is, of course, of the devil. These are the three enemies to our spiritual life. Exactly what are these enemies and how do we protect ourselves against them?

THE FLESH

THE ENEMY

One of the enemies of our spiritual life is "the flesh." We use the word "flesh" of the soft substances between our bones and skin. In the Bible, it is used of the body, but it is used figuratively of the internal tendency toward sin. Consider Romans 7: "For we know that the law is spiritual, but I am carnal, sold under sin. For what I am doing, I do not understand. For what I will to do, that I do not practice; but what I hate, that I do. If, then, I do what I will not to do, I agree with the law that *it is* good. "But now, *it is* no longer I who do it, but sin that dwells in me. For I know that in me (that is, in my flesh) nothing good dwells; for to will is present with me, but *how* to perform what is good I do not find. For the good that I will *to do*, I do not do; but the evil I will not *to do*, that I practice. Now if I do what I will not *to do*, it is no longer I who do it, but sin that dwells in me. I find then a law, that evil is present with me, the one who wills to do good. For I delight in the law of God according to the inward man. But I see another law in my members, warring against the law of my mind, and bringing me into captivity to the law of sin which is in my members. O wretched man that I am! Who will deliver me from this body of death? I thank God; through Jesus Christ our Lord! So then, with the mind I myself serve the law of God, but with the flesh the law of sin" (Rom. 7:14-25).

In this passage, the enemy of the spiritual life is the flesh. The Greek word translated "carnal" (Rom. 7:14) comes from the word for "flesh" and means "fleshly, carnal, sensual." To be "carnal" is to be "under the power of the flesh" (Hodge). The flesh is the tendency to sin. Paul says, "Sin dwells in me" (Rom. 7:17) and adds "in me (that is, in my flesh) nothing good dwells" (Rom. 7:18). In other words, the tendency to sin dwells in the flesh (see also Rom. 7:20). Also, the flesh serves the law of sin (Rom. 7:25).

The problem is not a lack of knowledge, nor is it a lack of desire. Paul says he knows what is right and desires to do it! (Rom. 7:19, 22). The desire to do what is right was so strong he "hated" the wrong that he did (Rom. 7:15). The problem is the sin principle within every believer.

Here is a test to see if you are living according to the flesh. "Now the works of the flesh are evident, which are: adultery, fornication, uncleanness, licentiousness, idolatry, sorcery, hatred, contentions, jealousies, outbursts of wrath, selfish ambitions, dissensions, heresies, envy, murders, drunkenness, revelries, and the like; of which I tell you beforehand, just as I also told you in time past, that those who practice such things will not inherit the kingdom of God" (Gal. 5:19-21). Anytime you manifesting of these characteristics, you are living according to flesh.

THE DEFENSE
Paul says, "There is therefore now no condemnation to those who are in Christ Jesus who do not walk according to the flesh but according to the Spirit" (Rom. 8:1). The word translated "condemnation" is only used three times in the New Testament (Rom. 5:16, 18; 8:1). It means the punishment following sentence, penal servitude. Paul is saying that the freedom from the servitude of sin comes by walking in the Spirit. The words "according to" mean the norm or the standard by which something is done. Believers can walk according to the standard of the flesh, which is the sin principle in them (Rom. 7:14, 23, 25), or they can live by the standard of the Holy Spirit (Rom. 8:1).

Paul explains, "For those who live according to the flesh set their minds on the things of the flesh, but those who live according to the Spirit the things of the Spirit. For to be carnally minded *is* death, but to be spiritually minded *is* life and peace" (Rom. 8:5-6). Believers can be either spiritually-minded or carnally-minded (Rom. 8:6). The Greek word translated "set their minds" includes the thinking, the will, and even the emotions (see commentaries by Godet and Hodge). Cranfield, another commentator, says it also includes one's outlook, assumptions, values, desires, and purposes. To set the mind on the flesh is to be oriented to or be governed by the things of the flesh.

Those whose inner being, their minds, choices, and feelings are focused on, oriented or governed by the things of the Holy Spirit will conduct their lives according to the Spirit. The things of the Spirit are the words of God (1 Cor. 2:12-14), especially the things about Christ (Jn. 16:13-15). Those whose emotions delight in the Lord, whose minds meditate on the Word of God, and whose wills choose to do what it says by depending on the Holy Spirit, will be living according to the Spirit with the result that they will be experiencing life and peace instead of death (Rom. 8:6). The life is the experience of God (Rom. 5:18; 6:4, 10; 7:4, 6; 8:2; see also Jn. 10:10). The peace is the resolution of the intense warfare and defeat described in Romans 7 and an inward feeling of harmony and tranquility that results.

How does living according to the Spirit prevent sin? In Galatians, Paul says, "I say then: Walk in the Spirit, and you shall not fulfill the lust of the flesh. For the flesh lusts against the Spirit, and the Spirit against the flesh; and these are contrary to one another so that you do not do the things that you wish" (Gal 5:16-17). The sinful tendency within the believer and the Holy Spirit within the believer are mutually exclusive, with the result that you do not do the things that you desire to do. Walking in the Spirit automatically excludes the fulfillment of sinful desires. This is the principle of replacement (see the chapter on "The Pattern of the Spiritual Life").

Here is a test to see if you are living according to the Spirit: "But the fruit of the Spirit is love, joy, peace, longsuffering, kindness, goodness, faithfulness, gentleness, self-control. Against such there is no law" (Gal. 5:22-23).

In simple terms, in essence, the flesh is that part of us that says, "Don't obey God; sin. Don't live your life in fellowship with Him; live your life apart from Him." As Burger King says, "Have it your way." The all-wise King of Kings says, "Do it My way."

THE WORLD

THE ENEMY

Another of our spiritual enemies is "the world." When we hear the word "world," we think of the earth. The Greek word translated "world" means "order, world, earth, universe." In the New Testament, it is used of 1) the created universe (Jn. 1:10), 2) mankind (Jn. 3:16; 1 Jn. 2:2), 3) the ordered system that is the opposite of and opposed to God (Jn. 15:18, 19; Jas. 4:4; 1 Jn. 2:15). The enemy of our spiritual life is that system the leaves God out, is opposite of God, and/ or is opposed to God.

John says, "Do not love the world or the things in the world. If anyone loves the world, the love of the Father is not in him. For all that is in the world; the lust of the flesh, the lust of the eyes, and the pride of life; is not of the Father but is of the world" (1 Jn. 2:15-16). The phrase "the love of the Father" means love *for* the father. By saying "love for the Father" instead of "love for God," John is pointing to the duty of the believers as *children* of God. If believers love the world, the love for the Father is not in them as the controlling factor in their life. To love the world is to venerate and value, cherish and choose that which is opposite to God.

John identifies the individual components of the world. First is the lust of the flesh. The Greek word rendered "lust" means "desire," not necessarily sexual desire, just desire. The lust of the flesh refers to a desire for sinful (probably sensual) pleasure, especially sexual pleasure. The lust of the eye consists of desires that come through, or are motivated by the eye. In other words, it is the desire to have what one sees. The thought is covetousness and greed aroused by what is seen. The last is the pride of life. The Greek word rendered "life" is not the normal word for life in the New Testament. This one means "period of life, course of life, livelihood." It refers to the means by which life is sustained. Thus, "the pride of life" refers to a proud, boastful, arrogant attitude concerning one's possessions or position, station or status. All three phrases describe the lifestyle that is opposite to and is opposed to God.

In a sense, the world wants pleasure, possessions, and power. The various world systems, the political world, the business world, the sports world, the religious world are about pleasure, possessions, and power apart from God. Those are the enemies of the spiritual life because if you live for those things, you will not be walking with the Lord.

People of the world seek pleasures that have diminishing returns. Each experience becomes less and less thrilling. It requires more to produce the same effect. Such pleasures are like a drug, which becomes less and less effective.

How foolish to seek pleasure in things that offer diminishing returns. People of the world seek possessions that wear out like a pair of shoes.

Robert Burns wrote:

> Pleasures are like poppies spread
> You seize the flower, its bloom is shed
> Or like the snow falls in the river,
> A moment white—then melts forever

THE DEFENSE

Paul writes, "Do not be conformed to this world, but be transformed by the renewing of your mind" (Rom. 12:2). Instead of being molded into the shape of this age, the believer should be transformed from the inside out by the renewing of the mind.

This is, no doubt, a reference to the spiritual-mindedness spoken of in Romans 8:6. As was pointed earlier in this chapter, the word "mind" in Romans 8 includes the mind, emotions, and the will. It also includes one's outlook, assumptions, values, desires, and purposes. As the mind and the heart and will of believers are fixed and focused on the Word of God in general, and Christ in particular, they are transformed more and more into Christ-likeness (see 2 Cor. 3:18, the only other place in Paul's writing where the word "transformed" appears). Such a person is said to have the mind of Christ (1 Cor. 2:16).

THE DEVIL

THE ENEMY

The third great enemy of our spiritual life is Satan. Satan's downfall was pride (1 Tim. 3:6). Satan would like to rule instead of God; he wants to replace God! In order to accomplish that end, he would like to keep people from knowing the Lord and those who do know the Lord from getting close to Him and serving Him. He would like to destroy every believer's walk with the Lord. Peter compares him to a roaming, roaring lion seeking whom he may devour, a word that means consume (1 Pet. 5:8).

We blame Satan for things he does not do. In an article on technology in general and traffic-light cameras in particular, Craig Ferguson says, "At the dawn of the Industrial Revolution, a group of weavers in England strongly objected to new mechanized looms. They said that the technology was the work of the devil. They were wrong, of course. Mechanized looms were a great step forward. Now, traffic-light cameras—they're the work of the devil" (Craig Ferguson, "Stop the Upgrades!" *Parade Magazine*, March 21, 2010, p. 14). Some believers credit Satan with things that should be credited to the flesh.

Paul says, "We are not ignorant of his devices" (2 Cor. 2:11). Satan tempts believers to sin. He tempts us to pride (1 Tim. 3:6), to be hypocritical (Acts 5:1-4), to lie (Acts 5:3, 5), to sexual immorality (1 Cor. 7:5), etc. That is only the beginning. In the Scripture, Satan is pictured as an angel of light seeking to deceive (2 Cor. 11:14; see also 2 Tim. 4:1), as a snake, soliciting doubt as well as disobedience (Gen. 3:1-6), and as a roaring lion, seeking to destroy (1 Pet. 5:8). The danger is that believers will listen to the devil and replace God in their lives.

"Satan appears as an angel of light, Paul tells us. He fell because he wanted to be like God. Satan's finished product is often a church deacon or elder who lives a very righteous life but doesn't have much trust in God. Self-righteousness serves his purposes as well as unrighteousness. And as long the Evil One can lure us from God, he doesn't care how well-behaved we are" (Haddon Robinson, *The Solid Rock Construction Company*, p. 93).

THE DEFENSE

Paul says, "Put on the whole armor of God, that you may be able to stand against the wiles of the devil. For we do not wrestle against flesh and blood, but against principalities, against powers, against the rulers of the darkness of this age, against spiritual hosts of wickedness in the heavenly places. Therefore take up the whole armor of God, that you may be able to withstand in the evil day, and having done all, to stand. Stand therefore, having girded your waist with truth, having put on the breastplate of righteousness, and having shod your feet with the preparation of the gospel of peace; above all, taking the shield of faith with which you will be able to quench all the fiery darts of the wicked one. And take the helmet of salvation, and the sword of the Spirit, which is the word of God; praying always with all prayer and supplication in the Spirit, being watchful to this end with all perseverance and supplication for all the saints" (Eph. 6:11-18). Simply put, the armor consists of truth, righteousness, the gospel of peace, faith, and salvation. The weapons consist of the Word of God and prayer. When Jesus was tempted by the devil, He quoted Scripture (Mt. 4:11). When He was tempted to not do the will of God concerning the cross, He prayed (Mt. 26:39).

Assuming believers have put on the armor and are armed with the Word of God and prayer, they should not give the devil a foothold in their lives by committing sins such as lying and anger (Eph. 4:25-27). They should also be on a constant watch out for an attack, that is, a temptation (1 Pet. 5:8) and resist it when it comes (1 Pet. 5:9). This resistance is not done in our strength alone. We must first submit to God and, then, resist the devil (Jas. 4:7). We do all things through Christ who gives us the strength to do what God tells us to do (Phil. 4:13).

Putting on the Armor of God, which includes truth and righteousness, is becoming Christ-like.

SUMMARY

The enemies of the spiritual life are: 1) the flesh, which says disobey God, 2), the world, which says oppose God, and 3) the devil, who says replace God. The way to protect yourself is: 1) to be spiritually-minded, 2) walk according to the Spirit, and 3) put on the armor of God. In short, don't exclude God; make sure you always include Him.

The flesh, the world, and the devil work together. James 3:15 says there is a wisdom (singular) that comes from below and lumps all three together. Someone has said, "Satan is the salesman; the world is the candy store, and the flesh is the desire for sweets." For example, sexual immorality is one of the works of the flesh (Gal. 5:19). Part of the world system is the lust of the flesh, which includes sexual immorality (1 Jn. 2:16) and Satan can tempt to sexual immorality (1 Cor. 7:5). Sexual immorality, then, is fleshly, worldly, and devilish.

The essence of the flesh, the world, and the devil is to leave God out of your life. Worldly wisdom is self-seeking (Jas. 3:14, 16). In other words, it leaves out the Lord.

The defense against the flesh, the world, and the devil is to include the Lord in all of your attitudes and activities. Live your life as unto the Lord. Live according to the Word of God and in dependence on the God of the Word. Simply put, include the Lord.

Once upon a mountain top, three little trees stood and dreamed of what they wanted to become when they grew up. The first little tree looked up at the stars and said: "I want to hold treasure. I want to be covered with gold and filled with precious stones. I'll be the most beautiful treasure chest in the world!" The second little tree looked out at the small stream trickling by on its way to the ocean. "I want to be traveling mighty waters and carrying powerful kings. I'll be the strongest ship in the world!" The third little tree looked down into the valley below where busy men and women worked in a busy town. It said, "I don't want to leave the mountain top at all. I want to grow so tall that when people stop to look at me, they'll raise their eyes to heaven and think of God. I will be the tallest tree in the world."

Years passed. The rain came, the sun shone, and the little trees grew tall. One day three woodcutters climbed the mountain. The first woodcutter looked at the first tree and said, "This tree is beautiful. It is perfect for me." With a swoop of his shining ax, the first tree fell. "Now I shall be made into a beautiful chest. I shall hold wonderful treasure!" the first tree said. The second woodcutter looked at the second tree and said, "This tree is strong. It is perfect for me." With a swoop of his shining ax, the second tree fell. "Now I shall sail mighty waters!" thought the second tree. "I shall be a strong ship for mighty kings!" The third tree felt her heart sink when the last woodcutter looked her way. She stood straight and tall and pointed bravely to heaven. But the woodcutter never even looked up. "Any kind of tree will do for me," he muttered. With a swoop of his shining ax, the third tree fell.

The first tree rejoiced when the woodcutter brought her to a carpenter's shop, but the carpenter fashioned the tree into a feed box for animals. The once beautiful tree was not covered with gold, nor with treasure. She was coated with sawdust and filled with hay for hungry farm animals. The second tree smiled when the woodcutter took her to a shipyard, but no mighty sailing ship was made that day. Instead, the once strong tree was hammered and sawed into a simple fishing boat. She was too small and too weak to sail on an ocean or even a river; instead, she was taken to a little lake. The third tree was confused when the woodcutter cut her into strong beams and left her in a lumberyard. "What happened?" the once tall tree wondered. "All I ever wanted was to stay on the mountain top and point to God."

Many, many days and nights passed. The three trees nearly forgot their dreams. One night, golden starlight poured over the first tree as a young woman placed her newborn baby in the feedbox. "I wish I could make a cradle for him," her husband whispered. The mother squeezed his hand and smiled as the starlight shone on the smooth and the sturdy wood. "This manger is beautiful," she said. And suddenly the first tree knew he was holding the greatest treasure in the world.

One evening a tired traveler and his friends crowded into the old fishing boat. The traveler fell asleep as the second tree quietly sailed out into the lake. Soon a thundering and thrashing storm arose. The little tree shuddered. She knew she did not have the strength to carry so many passengers safely through with the wind and the rain. The tired man awakened. He stood up, stretched out his hand, and said, "Peace." The storm stopped as quickly as it had begun. And suddenly the second tree knew he was carrying the king of heaven and earth.

One Friday morning, the third tree was startled when her beams were yanked from the forgotten woodpile. She flinched as she was carried through an angry jeering crowd. She shuddered when soldiers nailed a man's hands to her. She felt ugly and harsh and cruel. On Sunday morning, when the sun rose and the earth trembled with joy beneath her, the third tree knew that God's love had changed everything. It had made the third tree strong. And every time people thought of the third tree, they would think of God. That was better than being the tallest tree in the world.

Instead of looking at the world and wanting possessions, pleasure, and position, saturate your mind and heart with the Word. Focus on the Lord. Depend on the Lord to transform you in a vessel filled with the Lord.

CHAPTER THIRTEEN

THE COUNTERFEITS OF THE SPIRITUAL LIFE

Sometime ago, as I was reading a commentary, I came across this fascinating statement. "When God's truth is rejected, the human mind invents a substitute" (Homer Kent Jr.). It seems to me that is what happens in the spiritual life of believers. Either not knowing the truth or rejecting the truth, some believers adopt a substitute spiritual life.

The most detrimental thing you can do to your spiritual life is to accept a counterfeit for the spiritual life. If you succumb to the world, the flesh, or the devil, your conscience convicts you. You may rationalize, but you know something is wrong. If, however, you have accepted a substitute for the spiritual life, it will be more difficult for you to realize you are on the wrong path. You don't just rationalize; you can actually be proud of where you are spiritually. The archenemy of the spiritual life is a false spirituality.

Imagine how you would feel if you had unknowingly accepted a counterfeit $100 bill. Well, you may have accepted a counterfeit spirituality without realizing it. We need to rip off the disguises of counterfeits that pass off as spirituality. Make sure you have the real thing. To cover all the forms of counterfeit spiritually would take a book, but the most basic forms are explained by Paul in Colossians.

Paul begins by saying, "You are complete in Him" (Col. 2:10). He goes on to say that believers are "buried with Him in baptism, in which you also were raised with *Him* through faith in the working of God" (Col. 2:12) and "being dead in your trespasses and the uncircumcision of your flesh, He has made alive together with Him" (Col. 2:13). This is a condensed form of Romans 6 (see the chapter on "The Foundation of the Spiritual Life"). Then, he discusses three types of counterfeit spirituality.

LEGALISM

THE PROBLEM

Legalism is the doctrine which teaches that one must keep the Mosaic Law to be right with God. Paul says, "Therefore let no one judge you in food or in drink, or regarding a festival, or a new moon or Sabbaths" (Col. 2:16).

Food and drink are references to the Mosaic dietary laws concerning clean and unclean food (Lev. 10:9; 11:34, 36; Num. 6:3). The false teachers at Colosse probably went far beyond the Mosaic Law, as did the Pharisees. They probably forbade wine and animal food altogether (Lightfoot; 1 Tim. 4:2-3). At any rate, the idea is that keeping the Mosaic dietary laws is the way to be spiritual.

There are people today who teach that to be spiritual you must live by the Mosaic dietary laws. They even go beyond the dietary laws in the Old Testament and say that you should not eat meat. Seventh-Day Adventists are vegetarians. They eat hamburgers made of soybeans and called them "protein burgers." Being a vegetarian for health reasons is one thing, but abstaining from meat does not make you spiritual.

Festival, a new moon, and Sabbaths are references to the annual, monthly, and weekly holy days on the Jewish calendar. The festivals were Passover, Pentecost, and Tabernacles (Ex. 23:14-18). The new moon marked the observance of the lunar calendar (Num. 10:10; 28:11; 1 Sam. 20:18). It was a day of rest, fellowship, worship, and eating. The Sabbath is an obvious reference to the weekly observance of Saturday. On that day, Israel did not work, but rested and remembered the divine work of creation and her covenant relationship with God (Ex. 20:8-11; 31:12-18). Again, the idea is if you keep the holy days, you will be spiritual.

There are people who insisted on the observance of Saturday as the Sabbath. There is a denomination called "The Seventh Day Baptist General Conference." Their website says, "From our first church in America, founded in Newport, Rhode Island, in 1671, until today, Seventh Day Baptists have been a Christ-centered, Bible-believing people with traditional family values. We have over seventy churches in North America and churches in over twenty countries." They also say, "Seventh Day Baptists are a covenant people based on the concept of regenerate membership, believer's baptism, congregational polity, and scriptural basis for belief and practice. Seventh Day Baptists have presented the Sabbath as a sign of obedience in a covenant relationship with God and not as a condition of salvation. They have not condemned those who do not accept the Sabbath but are curious at the apparent inconsistency of those who claim to accept the Bible as their source of faith and practice, yet have followed traditions of the church instead."

Another application of the word "Sabbath" involves morality. The Sabbath is part of the Ten Commandments. Some think that spirituality is in keeping the Ten Commandments. They equate spirituality with morality. They look at the Law and say, "I have not murdered anybody. I am not committing adultery. I am not a thief. Therefore, I am in good shape spiritually."

Morality is important, but morality can be a substitute for spirituality. Unsaved people can be moral, but, obviously, they are not "spiritual" in the biblical sense of the term.

THE SOLUTION
Paul says believers should not let anyone judge them concerning the specifics of the Law because it was "a shadow of things to come, but the substance is of Christ" (Col. 2:17). The rules of the Mosaic legislation were shadows of things to come. The Old Testament was a figure, a type, a picture. The reality is Jesus Christ.

Imagine you and a friend are standing in the parking lot on a bright sunny afternoon. Because of the position of the sun, your friend's body casts a shadow on the ground, but the two of you are so involved in the conversation you're not aware of it. At that point, someone comes up to you and says that you should be concentrating on the shadow instead of conversing with your friend. That, of course, is absurd, but that is exactly what the false teachers were saying.

Paul insists that believers are not under the Law. He says the Law has been nailed to the cross (Col. 2:14). The point is that spiritual life is fellowship with the Lord, not obedience to rules. If you are in fellowship with the Lord, you will be moral, but morality is not spirituality. If you focus on the rules and dutifully obey them, you may think you are spiritual, but in reality, that is a false spirituality. True spirituality is conformity to Christ.

When we were small, we were vaccinated to protect us from disease. A vaccination gives you a small amount of the disease so that you do not get the real thing. For some people, being moral vaccinates them against real spirituality.

MYSTICISM

THE PROBLEM
Next, Paul warns about mysticism. Webster defines mysticism as, "The doctrine or belief that direct knowledge of God, of spiritual truth, etc., is obtainable

through immediate intuition or insight, and in a way differing from ordinary sense perception or the use of logical reasoning." That seems to be what Paul has in mind when he says, "Let no one cheat you of your reward, taking delight in false humility and worship of angels, intruding into those things which he has not seen, vainly puffed up by his fleshly mind" (Col. 2:18).

They were "intruding into those things which they have not seen," that is, they were claiming mystical insights. They were claiming to have extra-biblical insight and from it they concluded that angels should be worshiped (Alford; Eadie). They were puffed up about their special knowledge, meaning they were inflated with conceit. Nevertheless, these teachers came in humility, but their humility was false and their pride was vain.

This kind of thing exists today in people who claim that they have an extra-biblical insight through an intuition or an impression they received from the Lord. They say things like "the Lord led me to _____." Or "the Lord spoke to me." They even sound humble. They say, "It's not me; it's the Lord in me." They quote Galatians 2:20, claiming they are crucified with Christ and it is Christ that lives through them.

THE SOLUTION

Paul insists, "Let no one cheat you of your reward" (Col. 2:18). Some interpret this to mean, "Don't rob me of the prize of the high calling of God in Christ Jesus." Believers do not need extra-biblical revelation. They need insight into the biblical revelation they have.

Furthermore, the spiritual life is not just the Lord doing something without the believer being involved. Galatians 2:20 does say we are crucified with Christ, but it also says "the *life* which *I* now live in the flesh *I* live by faith in the Son of God, who loved me and gave Himself for me." Furthermore, Paul teaches, "*I* can do all things through Christ who strengthens me" (Phil. 4:13), not Christ does all things through me. God works in us and *we* work out our salvation (Phil. 2:12-13).

The problem is their relationship to Jesus Christ. Paul goes on to say that they were "not holding fast to the Head, from whom all the body, nourished and knit together by joints and ligaments, grows with the increase which is from God" (Col. 2:19). The Greek term translated "holding fast" describes a firm grip, a tenacious hold. The Head, of course, is Jesus Christ. Not holding to the head is profoundly serious, because Christ, as Head, is the source of nourishment and growth. The body, that is, the church, is joined to the Head by joints and ligaments. When every member is nourished (supplied with strength) and knitted together (united), there is growth. It is a growth that comes from God. The false teachers, without this contact with Christ, could not possibly contribute to the growth of the church.

There are those who claim to have had a revelation or an experience and they think that the revelation or experience makes them spiritual. The truth is that they are proud of their experience and want you to have it so you can be as spiritual as they are. Beware.

What sounds like spirituality may not be. Dr. Samuel Chetti tells of going to Durban, where he was taken to a Hindu temple. To his great surprise, the Hindus were singing the Christian song, "I Love You, Lord." They were using our song, but they were not singing about our Lord.

ASCETICISM

THE PROBLEM

Part of the false teaching threatening the Christians at Colosse was asceticism. Webster defines asceticism as the doctrine that "through self-torture or self-denial one can discipline himself to reach a high state spiritually or intellectually." That is what Paul is talking about when he says, "Therefore, if you died with Christ from the basic principles of the world, why, as though living in the world, do you subject yourselves to regulations" (Col. 2:20).

As in Colossians 2:8, the expression the "basic principles of the world" means "basic elements," that is, the material and the external, that which is evident to the senses, the visible and the material in contrast to the spiritual and invisible. The regulations (Col. 2:21) that Paul is speaking of here are man-made mandates (Col. 2:22). These ascetic restrictions were man-made rules imposed as a means of gaining favor with God.

In the early centuries of church history, asceticism existed in extreme forms. In the third and fourth centuries, people starved themselves until they became emaciated. To even bathe the body was thought to be sinful. During this period, it was not uncommon to neglect the body to the point of it becoming a breeding place for lice. One author speaks of lice dropping from people as they walked, which was considered a sign of special holiness.

Milder forms of asceticism exist today. Some Christians have a list of things not to do in order to be spiritual. Some have a list of the "filthy five," or the "sinful six," or the "nasty nine," or the "dirty dozen."

THE SOLUTION

Paul gives three reasons why asceticism should be rejected. In the first place, these restrictions do not apply to Christians. As Paul says in verse 20, "If you died with Christ from the basic principles of the world" (Col. 2:20a). In the Greek text, "if" is a first class condition, which means it should be translated "since." When believers trust Jesus Christ, they are buried with Him by baptism, and thus die to sin (Rom. 6:2), self (2 Cor. 5:14, 15), the law (Rom. 7:6), and the world (Col. 2:20; also Gal. 6:14). At conversion, the connection with the basic principles of the world of legal and ascetic ordinances is severed. When freed from prison, prisoners are no longer subject to the rules of the prison, so why should they put themselves back under prison rules? Those restrictions no longer apply.

Furthermore, the prohibitive lists are the types of things "which all concern things which perish with the using" (Col. 2:22a). No doubt the list included certain foods that were not to be eaten (see "do not taste" in Col. 2:21). Asceticism often leads to being a vegetarian to be spiritual. Paul argues that these are the kinds of things that perish when they are used.

Secondly, these restrictions are of human origin. Paul says that they are "according to the commandments and doctrines of men" (Col. 2:22b; see Mt. 15:9). In the Greek text, the two words "commandments" and "doctrines" are closely linked together. Both describe the same ascetic prohibitions. Paul's point is that all such regulations have their origin in the will and words of men.

Thirdly, the restrictions are ineffective. Paul says, "These things indeed have an appearance of wisdom in self-imposed religion, false humility, and neglect of the body, but are of no value against the indulgence of the flesh" (Col. 2:23). Paul grants that this list of man-made regulations has a show of wisdom. The ascetic rules masquerade as wisdom. On the surface, they seem to be reasonable and wise, but what seems to be reasonable is only an appearance of wisdom. In reality, they are expressions of self-imposed worship.

People practicing the neglect of the body may appear to be humble, but their humility is a false humility. While parading under the guise of humility, asceticism actually pampers human pride, but perhaps the most damaging and damning blow Paul makes at ascetic practices is that they are of no value against the indulgence of the flesh. All of the restrictions people put on the body are not able to prevent them from sinning. Thus, asceticism is ineffective; it simply does not work. Neglecting the body may have an appearance of wisdom, humility, and spirituality, but in the final analysis, asceticism is not able to prevent sin.

Eadie puts it like this, "A man might whip and fast himself into a walking skeleton, and yet the spirit within him might have all of its lust unconquered, for all it had lost was only the ability to gratify them. To place a fetter on a robber's hand will not cure him of covetousness, though it may disqualify him from actual theft. To seal up the swearer's mouth will not pluck profanity out of his heart, though it may, for the time, prevent him from taking God's name in vain. To lacerate the flesh almost to suicide merely incapacitates it for indulgence, but does not extirpate sinful desires. Its air of superior sanctity is only pride in disguise—it has but a 'show of wisdom' and is not."

SEEK SPIRITUAL THINGS

The solution is to reject asceticism and seek spiritual things. Thus far, Paul has told the Colossians what to avoid and reject; he now tells them what to put in its place. He gives two commands (see "seek" in Col. 3:1 and "set" in Col. 3:2), and reasons why these commands should be obeyed (see "for" in Col. 3:3).

SEEK

Paul begins by saying, "If then you were raised with Christ, seek those things which are above, where Christ is, sitting at the right hand of God" (Col. 3:1). Do not seek the things on the earth (Col. 3:2); that is, the legalistic, mystical, and ascetic practices of the false teachers, as well as sins.

Seek the things above. Believers are in Christ (Col. 3:3), who is sitting at the right hand of God. It is only logical that they would be seeking heavenly things. The kinds of things that Paul has in mind are probably the list of virtues given in Colossians 3:12-17.

SET YOUR MIND

The second command Paul gives is: "Set your mind on things above, not on things on the earth" (Col. 3:2). To set the mind on something is more than just thinking about it. The concept involves the whole bent of the inner nature, including the mind, the heart, and the will (see "set your affections" in the KJV). The inner self is not to be directed toward earthly things, that is, the rules, revelations, and regulations mentioned above, and the list of sins, which follow in this passage. Rather, the inner self is to be directed toward Jesus Christ and spiritual things.

SUMMARY

The counterfeits of a biblical spiritual life are legalism, mysticism, and asceticism. The spiritual life does not consist of rules, revelations (visions, impressions), or regulations; it is a relationship with Jesus Christ.

Because of what believers are, have, and will be in Christ, they should reject all false views of spirituality and seek spiritual things. Christ has met every spiritual need. The believer is complete in Him, and thus should seek Him and spiritual things. To put the same thing another way, what has legalism done for you that you should live by rules? What has mysticism done for you that you should live by revelations? What has asceticism done for you that you should live by regulations?

According to a Persian legend, a fabulous bird of the East was supposed to bring good fortune to all who came under the shadow of its wings. One day the king was riding along in royal splendor surrounded by his courtiers when suddenly the huge creature was spotted flying a short distance away. All the attendants except one immediately rushed to get under the bird's shadow. The monarch, surprised that this servant had not joined the others, inquired, "Why didn't you go with them?" The courtier responded, "Why should I go running after some old bird when I can enjoy the presence of my king?" The ruler was so moved and pleased by his servant's devotion that he promoted him to prime minister of the realm.

CHAPTER FOURTEEN

THE BENEFITS OF THE SPIRITUAL LIFE

Becoming a Christian does not solve all the problems of life. In a sense, living a spiritual life makes life even more difficult. Jesus said, "In the world you will have tribulation" (Jn. 16:33). Paul said, "We must through many tribulations enter the kingdom of God" (Acts 14:22). Believers have the world, the flesh, and the devil as enemies, trial as obstacles, and counterfeits as substitutes. If that is the case, what are the benefits of a spiritual life?

There are many advantages to living a spiritual life. One of the major ones is the salvation of the soul. In the New Testament, the expression "the salvation of the soul" is not speaking about going to heaven by and by; it is a reference to something in the here and now.

When Dr. Earl Radmacher stood to speak, the first words to fall from his lips were, "You are looking at an unsaved preacher." Since there is no doubt that he knows the Lord, what could he possibly mean by that?

As all theologians recognize, *the New Testament uses the word "save" in three different ways: salvation from the penalty of sin, salvation from the power of sin, and salvation from the presence of sin.* Salvation from sin's penalty is immediate. It is secured by Christ's death (Rom. 1:16; Acts 28:18; 16:31; Rom. 10:10; 1 Cor. 15:2; 2 Tim. 1:9). Salvation from sin's power is continuous. It is by Christ's life (Heb. 7:25; Rom. 5:9; Jas. 1:23; 1 Tim. 4:6; Phil. 2:12). Salvation from sin's presence is prospective. It is at Christ's coming (Rom. 13:11; Heb. 9:28; Phil. 3:20; 1 Thess. 5:8). The first is past, the second is present, and the third is future. Paul speaks of having been saved (Eph. 2:8), being saved in the present (1 Cor. 1:18), and being saved in the future (Rom. 13:11).

Dr. Radmacher was not saying he was not justified, regenerated, or saved in the sense of being saved from the penalty of sin. He was acknowledging that, in the words of Paul, he was "being saved" (1 Cor. 1:18), that is, being saved from the power of sin. Hence, he could dramatically, but actually, say that he was an unsaved preacher, meaning there are still times when he sins.

That is a clear and simple truth of the New Testament. The confusion concerns the expression "the salvation of the soul" (Jas. 1:21; 1 Pet. 1:9). When most believers hear about the soul being saved they think about salvation from the penalty of sin, but in the New Testament, the salvation of the soul is a reference to being saved from the power of sin. The Greek word translated "soul" means "soul, life." Actually, it is a word with multiple meanings, but its basic meaning is simply "life." In that sense, humans (Gen. 2:7 KJV; the NKJV says, "living being"), animals (Gen. 1:24, where "soul" is translated "living creature"), and fish (Rev. 16:3) have a soul, that is, they all have life. When Jesus said, that He laid down His life (Mk. 10:45), the Greek word He used for life is "soul."

In other words, it is possible to be "saved" (past tense, that is, from the power of sin), but from an eternal perspective lose one's life, that is, to spiritually waste it.

What are you doing with your life? Are you using for eternal profit? Or, from an eternal perspective, are you wasting it?

JESUS

THE REQUIREMENT FOR DISCIPLESHIP

Matthew records, "Then Jesus said to His disciples, 'If anyone desires to come after Me, let him deny himself, and take up his cross, and follow Me'" (Mt. 16:24). Notice, in this passage, Jesus addresses disciples. As we have seen, there is a difference between being a believer and being a disciple. A believer is a person who has trusted Jesus Christ for the gift of eternal life (Rom. 6:23; Eph. 2:8). Since Jesus paid for our sins, eternal life is without cost to us (Rom. 3:24; Rev. 22:17). A disciple, on the other hand, is a learner, which is the meaning of the Greek word translated "disciple." A learner is someone who is obeying Christ (Jn. 8:31; Lk. 14:26-27). So, in this passage, Jesus is speaking to those who are already saved; He is speaking to learners. That should be obvious from the fact that what He says here is not what people have to do to obtain eternal life; it is what they have to do to follow Him.

Jesus lays out the requirements for becoming a disciple, including desire, denial of yourself as the final authority for how to live your life, daily suffering (Lk. 9:23), and diligent obedience. To be a disciple you must desire to follow Christ, deny yourself (that is, chose to do God's will), and follow Christ, which means trusting Him and obeying Him.

THE REASON FOR DISCIPLESHIP

Jesus continues, "For whoever desires to save his life will lose it, but whoever loses his life for My sake will find it" (Mt. 16:25). This statement sounds like double talk. How can you lose something by saving it and find something by losing it?

To explain why people would want to deny themselves and suffer in following Him, Jesus uses an ordinary business concept (loss, gain, profit). What some think is a gain, turns out to be a loss. What they thought would be a loss ends up a gain. The loss is not a loss and the gain is not a gain (Alexander).

We naturally think that if we use our life to do what we want to do, that is gain; we have saved our life. Jesus is saying that is what you think, but if you do that, when life is over, you will discover that you lost your life, that is, you wasted it. On the other hand, we think if we do God's will ("for My sake"), we lose out on life. Jesus is saying that is what you think, but if you do that, when life is over, you will discover that you really saved it. It is the opposite of what we think. As children, we sang, "Finders keepers; losers weepers." Spiritually, it is "keepers weepers; losers finders."

Jesus explains ("for") the loss by asking two penetrating questions. "For what profit is it to a man if he gains the whole world, and loses his own soul? Or what will a man give in exchange for his soul?" (Mt. 16:26). Jesus contemplates the possibility of gaining the whole world and in the process losing one's life. The Greek word translated "soul" means "breath, life, soul." It is the same word that was translated "life" twice in the previous verse. Both times the word "soul" appears in this verse, it is the same Greek word translated "life" in the previous verse. Plummer says that "we must keep" the translation "life" throughout the passage (see Plummer on Lk. 9:25; see also the NKJV translation of Lk. 9:25). The issue here is about your physical life (Mt. 16:25).

Actually, Jesus is asking a question. The question is, "If a person gave his life to gain material possessions, what profit would he have?" The word "profit" indicates that Jesus is referring to rewards after this life is over; He is speaking about eternal reward (Mt. 16:27). It has been suggested that 1 Corinthians 13:3 is a "supplementary thought" to this passage (M'Neile).

Suppose a financial wizard was so shrewd he was able to gain all the material possessions of the whole world, but in doing so he lost his own life. To give your life to gain possessions may make dollars, but it does not make sense. Or imagine a politician who gained all the power in the world and in the process did nothing worthy of eternal value. What would be the lasting profit of his life?

Think of a young woman just having given birth to her first baby. As she lies in the hospital cuddling her newborn with the rapture of new motherhood on her face, I say to her, "How much do you want for your child?" She shows no interest. So I offer her the city of Los Angeles. She is not moved; she refuses the offer. I offer her the state of California, but she declines to seal the deal. Then, I offer her the entire United States, but she continues to refuse my proposal. Finally, I offer her the whole world. I can imagine her saying, "My baby is worth more to me than the whole world. No deal!" The life of that baby was of more value to her than the whole world. Likewise, from an eternal point of view, our life lived for Christ's sake is of more value than gaining the whole world. That is saving your life.

The Greek word translated "exchange" is about giving not receiving, so the meaning may be "what shall a man pay to get back his life, after he has forfeited it by sinning to get gain" (Plummer).

Jesus explains ("for") the gain: "For the Son of Man will come in the glory of His Father with His angels, and then He will reward each according to his works" (16:27). The Lord explains ("for") that He will come again, not as a sufferer, but as a judge to *reward* disciples according to their works. Toussaint sums it up, "Thus the disciples must endure suffering, and when the Son of Man comes in His glory, they will be rewarded." The rewards will be based on works (Ps. 62:12; Prov. 24:12).

Walvoord comments, "For the world, there is an immediate gain but ultimate loss: for the disciple, there is an immediate loss but an ultimate gain." Plummer observes, "The Author of their salvation must be made perfect by suffering (Heb. ii. 10), yet all needed to be taught that they themselves require suffering for their perfecting, and must be prepared for it and willing to endure it."

Barclay writes, "The man who selfishly hugs life to himself, the man whose first concern is his own safety, his own security and his own comfort, is in heaven's eyes the failure, however rich and successful and prosperous he may seem to be. The man who spends himself for others, and who lives life as a gallant adventure, is the man who receives heaven's praise and God's reward."

Early in the 20th century, an ad appeared in a London newspaper which read, "Men wanted for hazardous journey. Small wages, bitter cold, one month of complete darkness, constant danger. Safe return doubtful." The ad was placed by Sir Ernest Shackleton, the famous South Pole explorer. The response was overwhelming. Shackleton said that it was as if all the men of England wanted to go. They were will to suffer hardship for the adventure and future glory of going to the South Pole.

JAMES

James also speaks of saving your life: "Therefore lay aside all filthiness and overflow of wickedness, and receive with meekness the implanted word, which is able to save your souls" (Jas. 1:21). "Lay aside" literally means "put off." It was used of putting off a garment, like a coat. He uses two words to refer to sin: 1) filthiness and 2) overflow of wickedness. Filthiness means just that: dirty, filthy. It was used of a dirty, filthy, badly soiled shabby coat. Here it is used of moral defilement. "Wickedness" can mean either badness or malice. In the New Testament, it seems to mean malice, that is badness toward someone—spite or an attitude of getting even. That is probably the meaning here. What is to be laid aside is the abundance, the overflow, of sin, which is malice.

After laying aside sin, one is to receive the implanted Word. The "implanted word" (Jas. 1:21) is the word planted in a believer's life after the new birth. The Word is to be received with meekness. Meekness is not weakness. It is the picture of someone who has the strength of steel, but who has a teachable spirit.

James insists that such a process is able to save a person's soul. In this context, James is not talking about a sinner getting saved and going to heaven. He is talking about saints and sin. Sin is filthy; it gets people dirty, does damage and causes death (Jas. 1:15). The word translated "soul" means "life." James is saying the Word can save a believer's life from dirt, damage, and the death that sin causes if he or she receives it with a teachable spirit.

James has already talked about faith (Jas. 1:3) and he goes on to talk about obeying the word (Jas. 1:25). So, it is not too much to say that according to James, the way to save your life is by faith and obedience.

PETER

Peter speaks about saving your life: "receiving the end of your faith; the salvation of *your* souls" (1 Pet 1:9). Again, the Greek word translated "soul" means "life." The way the save your "life" is by trusting the Lord (1 Pet. 1:8) and obeying the Word (1 Pet. 2:1-2).

The Greek word rendered "receiving" means "to receive back." Hort says that the word "often in all Greek and always in the New Testament means not simply to receive, but to receive back, to get what has belonged to oneself and has been lost or else promised but kept back or to get what has come to be one's own by earning" (Hort, p. 47; also Mouton and Milligan, p. 354). It has "special reference to what is deserved or earned" (Selwyn). Hence, as believers trust God and rejoice in God even in the midst of trials, God is paying them back. They are earning the salvation of their life by faith and rejoicing. The revelation of that salvation awaits the coming of Christ (1 Pet. 1:5, 7).

SUMMARY

From an eternal perspective, one of the major benefits of living a spiritual life is that you will save your life from being wasted. If you live for yourself, you will lose your life, but if you live in faith and obedience to Christ, you will save your life.

Paul says, "For bodily exercise profits a little, but godliness is profitable for all things, having promise of the life that now is and of that which is to come" (1 Tim. 4:8). The spiritual life is profitable in this life and in the life to come. What does that mean?

TREASURE
Jesus said, "Lay up for yourselves treasures in heaven, where neither moth nor rust destroys and where thieves do not break in and steal" (1 Tim. 6:20). You cannot take it with you, but you can send it ahead.

AUTHORITY
In Luke 19, Jesus told a parable about a wealthy man, who left on a trip. Before his departure, he gave a mina (worth about four months' wages) to ten servants and told them to engage in business until he returned. When he returned, he gathered them together and asked for an accounting. The first to report had earned ten times what he had received. He was told, "Well done, good servant; because you been faithful in a very little, have authority over ten cities." The second to report had earned five times what he was given. He was told, "You will be over five cities." The third to report had an interesting story.

Here's the way Luke records it: "Then another came, saying, 'Master, here is your mina, which I have kept put away in a handkerchief. For I feared you because you are an austere man. You collect what you did not deposit, and reap what you did not sow" (Lk. 19:20-21). Jesus called him a "wicked servant." The master took the money he had given that servant and gave it to the man who had earned ten times what he had been given (Lk. 19:12-27).

The servants who believed what their master told them and did what they were told to do were rewarded with administrative responsibility. Likewise, those who lay up treasure in heaven will have an administrative role on the kingdom. *Crowns* Paul speaks of five different crowns.

- An Incorruptible Crown for self-control (1 Cor. 9:25)
- A Crown of Life for steadfastness in trials (Jas. 1:12; Rev. 2:10); faithfulness
- A Crown of Righteousness for steadfastness in service (2 Tim. 4:8); hope
- A Crown of Rejoicing for soul winning (1 Thess. 2:19).
- A Crown of Glory for shepherding (1 Pet. 5:4); love

When people die, those who remain ask, "What did they leave?" Those in heaven ask, "What did they send ahead?"

Peter teaches that we can have an abundant entrance into the kingdom. He writes, "But also for this very reason: giving all diligence; add to your faith virtue, faith virtue, to virtue knowledge, to knowledge self control, to self-control perseverance, to perseverance godliness, to godliness brotherly kindness, and to brotherly kindness love. For if these things are yours and abound, you will be neither barren nor unfruitful in the knowledge of our Lord Jesus Christ. For he who lacks these things is shortsighted, even to blindness, and has forgotten that he was purged from his old sins. Therefore, brethren, be even more diligent to make your calling and election sure, for if you do these things you will never stumble; For so an entrance will be supplied to you abundantly into the everlasting kingdom of our Lord and Savior Jesus Christ" (2 Pet. 1:5-11).

Do you feel that your life is in danger? I have been in several situations where I feared for my life. Many years ago, I was on a plane that suddenly began to fall out of the sky. The stewardess said that we dropped 50 feet; the engineer sitting next to me said it was 500 feet. Obviously, the pilot was able to pull out of the dive. I am here to tell about it, but at the time, I thought my life was in danger.

Once on the way to a speaking engagement, as I was driving through Detroit, I drove through a series of gunshots outside a bar. I don't know that any of the bullets were headed toward me, but I feared for my life. I have been mugged in South Central Los Angeles and was once in a bank that suddenly locked all the doors, because it had just been robbed. By the time I figured out what was going on, the robber had fled, but the experience didn't exactly make me feel safe in my own bank.

Have you ever feared for your life? Perhaps you should! You could live in the safest suburb or in a gated community and be in danger of losing your life. That is what Jesus taught, and James and Peter echoed.

John Wilkes Booth assassinated Abraham Lincoln when he was 27 years old. He fled from Washington and ended up hiding in a barn. When he was found, there was a gun battle in which Booth was shot. One account says, "Lying on the farmhouse porch, the blood pouring from the wound in his neck inflicted by Corbett and 'suffering the most excruciating agony a human being can know,' Booth struggled to speak. 'Tell mother I died for my country,' he gasped. 'I did what I thought was best.' Later, 'as the dawn was breaking into brilliant day, he indicated by a look, a feeble motion, that he wanted his paralyzed arms raised so he could see his hands. This was done, and he said, very faintly, as he looked at them: "Useless—useless!" Those were his last words. Whether he bemoaned the uselessness of his hands to fight for him, or the uselessness of their mad crime, God only knows, but he could not more accurately have epitomized his insane deed.

Will you get to the end of your life and look at what you have done and say, "Useless?" If you do not follow Christ in faith and obedience, that will be God's verdict on your life.

CHAPTER FIFTEEN

CONCLUSION

From a biblical point of view, a spiritual life begins by trusting Jesus Christ for the gift of eternal life. Eternal life is not just a life that lasts forever; it is God's kind of life. Therefore, the spiritual life begins having God's life in you (regeneration).

The *nature* of the spiritual life is spiritual growth from spiritual infancy to spiritual maturity in the context of a spiritual community. It is not being religious.

The *goal* is Christ-like maturity, which includes truth, righteousness, and justice on the one hand and love, grace, and mercy on the other hand, as well as a number of other characteristics, such as being meek and gentle, sensible and self-controlled, patient with people and enduring in trials. It is not external activities; it is internal Christ-likeness.

The *pattern* is putting off vices and putting on virtues. It involves the principle of replacement of vices with virtues and is a process of gradual growth over time, whereby little by little there are attitudinal and behavioral changes. Although some have a crisis in their lives that turns their attention toward a spiritual life, a crisis is not required. The spiritual life is a process.

The *requirement* for the spiritual life is a deep desire and determination to walk with the Lord and be like Him. It is a life of fellowship with God and His Son, Jesus Christ, as provided by God the Holy Spirit. It cannot be emphasized too strongly that the spiritual life is a relationship with the Lord. It is not living by rules and regulations.

The *power* for living a biblical spiritual life comes from knowing that you are united to Jesus Christ (the Baptism of the Holy Spirit), which means that the old you is dead and that you are a new person in Christ. You are alive to God.

The *means* of the spiritual life are the Word, faith, obedience, the Holy Spirit, fellowship, and trials. As believers contemplate the characteristics of

Christ in the Word (and as seen in others), believing what God says and obeying what God says by being dependant on the grace of God, the Holy Spirit transforms them. As believers become more and more spiritually minded, they more and more walk according to the Holy Spirit. Trials and fellowship with other believers (church) are part of the process. The spiritual life is not lived by letting God do everything; believers must be actively involved in the process. The motivation is love. We love Him, trust Him, and obey Him because He first loved us.

The *challenge* to the spiritual life is the trials of life.

The *enemies* of the spiritual life are the world, the flesh, and the devil.

The *counterfeits* of the spiritual life are legalism, mysticism, and asceticism.

The *benefits* of the spiritual life are in this life and in the life to come.

SUMMARY

As children of God believe and obey the Word of God by being dependent on the grace of God, they are more and more over time transformed by the Spirit of God into the image of the Son of God from glory to glory.

A biblical spiritual life is not about externals, such as rules, restrictions, and regulations. It is an inside job. It is not about activities such as Bible reading, meditation, prayer, and church attendance. It is an internal transformation.

What a glorious opportunity! Believers can be transformed into Christlikeness.

ABOUT THE AUTHOR

G. Michael Cocoris is a communicator. He possesses an ability to make even complicated subjects simple, clear, and practical. His breadth of experience has given him the ability to relate to a wide range of audiences. He has been an evangelist, conference speaker, adjunct professor, visiting lecturer, professor, author, pastor, and world traveler.

Mike received a Bachelor of Arts degree from Tennessee Temple University (1962), a Master of Theology degree from Dallas Theological Seminary (1966) and a Doctorate of Divinity from Biola University (1984).

While he was in seminary, Mike was Pastor of the First Baptist Church of Pattonville, Texas (1963-66), where he was ordained. From 1966 to 1974, he was an itinerant evangelist, speaking in churches, youth camps, conferences, service clubs, high schools, colleges, and seminaries thought-out the United States. For six summers he was the youth speaker at the Blue Water Camp and Conference Center, Wallaceburg, Ontario, Canada. In 1974, he became Vice President of EvanTell Inc. in Dallas, Texas and an adjunct Professor at Dallas Theological Seminary. He became Senior Pastor of the historic Church of the Open Door in 1979, first in downtown Los Angeles and later in Glendora, CA. While at the Church of the Open Door he had a daily radio broadcast that was heard on as many as 59 stations.

Besides writing numerous magazine articles, mainly for *Biblical Research Monthly*, Mike has authored several books including *Evangelism: A Biblical Approach, Lordship Salvation: Is it Biblical?, Seventy Years on Hope Street, The Salvation Controversy, and Repentance, the Most Misunderstood Word in the Bible*. In addition, he was a contributor to *The NKJV Study Bible* and *Nelson's New Illustrated Bible Commentary*.

Mike has spoken in more than 40 states, conducted tours to the Holy

Land, England, Europe, and China, has served on the board of four Christian organizations including a college and a university, and has been listed in *Who's Who in Religion*.

Since 1996, Mike has been the Pastor of The Lindley Church in Tarzana, CA and since 2006, he has been Professor of Bible at the Pacific International Theological Seminary in Alhambra, CA. He and his wife, Patricia, live in Santa Monica, CA.

CPSIA information can be obtained
at www.ICGtesting.com
Printed in the USA
FSHW011000260919
62356FS